# **Revelation**
# revealed

© Day One Publications 2005
First printed 2005

ISBN 1-903087-84-8

9 781903 087848 >

Unless otherwise stated, all Scripture quotations are from the
**New International Version** copyright © 1973, 1978, 1984

British Library Cataloguing in Publication Data available

Published by Day One Publications
Ryelands Road, Leominster, HR6 8NZ
☎ 01568 613 740 FAX 01568 611 473
email—sales@dayone.co.uk
web site—www.dayone.co.uk
North American—e-mail—sales@dayonebookstore.com
North American—web site—www.dayonebookstore.com

Designed by Steve Devane and printed by Gutenberg Press, Malta

**For Elaine,**
Whose continued love and understanding
is an ongoing revelation to me

# Introduction

R evelation is a closed book to many, and it ought not to be. Not only is it part of the word of God, it is also an immensely relevant book to Christians in every age.

This little study does not attempt a word-by-word analysis, nor a look at all the details. Rather, it should be seen as standing well back from a great painting, in an attempt to get the whole picture. Even then, some of what I have said will be controversial for some, but I hope all will find it helpful.

Like most preachers, I have many sources. A good friend once told me that if you copy from one person it is plagiarism; if you copy from many it is research. I am guilty, therefore, of much research here! Where possible, I have acknowledged help where it was given. But if you read a passage and think you heard a different preacher say something very similar, you probably did—and I was probably there, too.

In particular, though, I must acknowledge the tape ministry of Stuart Olyott, which has helped me through many a difficult passage. On several occasions I have followed his material very closely, and I am grateful to him for his permission to do so. On some important passages, though, I differed from him: it would be unfair, therefore, to blame him for my mistakes.

# Contents

Chapter 1

# Eyes of fire

Please read Revelation Chapter 1

T he book of Revelation is probably the most exciting book in the New Testament. Fast-moving drama, great persecutions, high suspense and vivid imagery all combine to make it a breath-taking read. It is an amazing book; if we study it properly we will sometimes almost burst to cry out 'Hallelujah' and then, at others, we will find our hearts wanting to break with love for the Lord who loves us.

## Beware neglect

It is strange, therefore, that many Christians only seem to have twenty-six books in their New Testament, with the book of Revelation being the neglected one. It is not the fault of the book! Instead, it is because there have been so many fanciful interpretations of Revelation over the years that the ordinary Christian just does not know what to make of it. So many charts and diagrams have been produced along with so many dogmatic statements about the man whose number is 666 that many of us have decided it is a book best left to the experts. Even the great nineteenth-century preacher Spurgeon commented 'There is a whole Book of Revelation which I do not understand,' and said 'Only fools and madmen are positive in their interpretations of the Apocalypse'[1] while Calvin, probably the greatest Bible commentator of them all, left Revelation untouched in his New Testament commentaries.

But in spite of the hesitance of such great men, I believe that Revelation is by far the easiest book in the New Testament to understand! Easy, that is, if we will content ourselves with getting the general picture. If, on the other hand, we want to identify every horn on every head of the Beast from the Sea (Revelation 13) then we will have enormous difficulty. Even if we manage it, no-one else will ever agree with us. If we forget that Revelation is full of symbolism, or if we become obsessed with the meaning of individual symbols, we will soon find ourselves lost in the by-ways of a thousand fabulous interpretations. More importantly, we will inevitably miss the point of the book.

## Beware blasphemy

In Greek, the very first word of the book is 'apocalypse' which means a revelation or an unveiling, and it has given its name to apocalyptic literature—a style that was very popular in the first century AD. It is a type of literature that makes much use of symbolism and symbolic numbers; parts of Daniel and Zechariah are other Biblical examples of 'apocalyptic' literature. Some readers of Revelation have been so confused by its imagery (and so ignorant of apocalypse as a literary style) that they assume the book makes no sense. They may explain its 'nonsense' in various ways; for example, John has been described as a drug-addict under the influence of sacred mushrooms, or a madman whose last connection with sanity has been broken. It never seems to occur to such readers that the fault might be theirs.

We do not need to answer such unbelief in detail. It is enough for us to know the source of the book; that source is Jesus Christ himself, and God the Father. The Father has given a revelation to his Son Jesus Christ, who has sent an angel to make known (literally 'signify' which means 'to make known by signs') that revelation to the apostle John. In turn, John makes it known to us, so that we may receive a blessing from it (1:1–3). Reading the book is meant to be a blessing, not an intellectual puzzle.

The purpose of the revelation John is given is to show us, the servants of Jesus, what must soon take place (1:1). Again, we note that it is meant to make something known, not to cover it up. Since Revelation is a book full of vivid word-pictures, it is appropriate that the word translated 'show' here has as its primary meaning 'to expose to the eyes'. John wants us to catch a glimpse of the future, and so does John's Lord.

There are several different ways of understanding the whole book. The *preterist* believes that all the symbols and events refer to things that were current at the time John wrote. The *historicist* sees John as presenting a chronological history of the world from his own day to the second coming. The *futurist*, however, insists that all the book (at least from chapter 4) is still future, and speaks only of the last few years before the second coming.

Which is right? John speaks of 'what must soon take place' (verse 1), but how soon is soon? When will the things revealed here begin? The answer is: they have already begun. The opening verse of the book makes it clear that what is revealed cannot just refer to the years before the very end of the world, as some interpreters imagine. That would not only make Revelation largely irrelevant to its first readers (and perhaps—who knows—to us, too) but it would also stretch the meaning of 'soon' beyond any reasonable limits. But the historicist and the preterist have their problems, too. So the view taken here sees Revelation as describing what will happen throughout the whole period from the first to the second comings of Jesus—but not in chronological order. We do not have to work out 'where we are' in Revelation, because the whole book describes our own age and every age.

## The key

The key to understanding Revelation is to see that its twenty-two chapters consist of an introduction (Chapter One) and seven sections. The first section—the letters to the seven churches—have lessons that are always relevant for every church in every age. Each of the other six sections deals with the whole sweep of history from the first coming of our Lord Jesus to his final return in glory. They cover the whole of human history from incarnation to return, and view the period from different perspectives. That is, the visions of each section are parallel to one another, not consecutive. I will try to demonstrate that as we proceed, but it is vital to grasp it right at the beginning. Many of the mistakes in interpreting Revelation come from a failure to grasp this point.

The purpose of this present book is to give us enough understanding of Revelation to approach it without fear, and to take encouragement from it as we are meant to. It is an overview, not a commentary. Imagine looking at some great old painting. If you are an expert, you might want to go up very close. You would want to examine the brush-strokes of the artist, his use of colour and of light and shade to great effect. But if the Book of Revelation were that painting, we would be those standing well back to get the overall picture. Other approaches are useful, but until we know what the picture is about we really cannot progress any further. There is a great promise for those who read Revelation: 'Blessed is the one who reads the words of this prophecy, and blessed are those who hear it and take to heart what is written in it, because the time is near' (1:3). We are in search of that blessing.

## Background
No-one is absolutely sure when the book was written; perhaps as late as 95 AD, but some think as early as 65 or 70 AD. The later date is more likely; Domitian was emperor of Rome by then, and he was the first one who banished, rather than killed, Christian people. But whenever it is John, the disciple Jesus loved, (which is how John refers to himself five times in his gospel) is in exile on the isle of Patmos. Many of his fellow disciples have already been put to death for their faith. John though is a living martyr, a living sacrifice for the word of God and the testimony of Jesus (1:9). It is the Lord's day—the first day of the week, when Christians commemorate the resurrection of Jesus—and John is 'in the Spirit' (1:10). We may be sure that even in his exile John is delighted to do all he can, each Sunday, to worship God and rest from his usual labours. Neither bitterness about his captivity nor complaint about the way God is treating him is allowed to interrupt his worship. While he is in the Spirit a Voice speaks to him and the wilderness of Patmos becomes a gateway to heaven as he is given a fresh vision of Jesus his Lord. Surely a vision of that Lord will do much to ease any pain he may be enduring as an exile of the emperor.

One of the sad signs of decline in Christian living in our day is a carelessness about Sundays. The Lord's Day is a great provision, a real blessing from God, and we should see it as a gift, not a burden. It is a good thing to be 'in the Spirit' on his day. That little phrase ('in the Spirit') may help to answer a thousand questions about the fourth commandment: we should not ask 'can I do this or that?' (or even 'why *can't I* do this or that?') but instead 'will this or that allow me to be 'in the Spirit'? Will it help or hinder my fellowship with God and his people?' Sunday is a day of consecration; and somehow John, though sentenced to Patmos—a labour camp, where the enemies of the Roman Emperor, Domitian, were sent to work in the quarries—finds time for worship and contemplation.

So, John is worshipping, and while he worships, he has a vision—a vision of a man he knows and remembers so well. The purpose of Sunday is the same as the purpose of Revelation: we miss the point of both unless we 'see Jesus.' The phrase 'The revelation of Jesus Christ' (1:1) could mean 'the revelation that Jesus Christ gave.' But equally, and more likely, it can mean that Jesus is the *object* of the revelation given; it is Jesus Christ who is being revealed. We miss the point of the whole book if we miss this!

John sees a vision of the Lord Jesus. He has walked with this man, talked with him, eaten with him: but now he sees as never before the *glory* of Jesus. At least once before John had caught a glimpse of that glory (see Matthew 17:1–8). This time words fail him as he tries to describe for us the glory of the vision of the Lord Jesus. The word picture is thrilling, marvellous, amazing; but it is the first of many such word pictures that would be impossible to draw. We must take note though of the eyes of blazing fire, (1:14). When we come to chapters two and three we will see there the Lord Jesus speaking to seven churches in Asia Minor. It becomes clear very quickly that Jesus knows all there is to know about them: these blazing eyes have missed nothing. Our Lord Jesus is, after all, the 'God who sees' (Genesis 16:13).

But those words to the churches are a little way off yet; for the moment, John sees the glory of the Lord and immediately falls at his feet as though dead (verse 17). Like Isaiah before him who saw the glory of Jesus (see Isaiah 6 and John 12:41), the sight is too much for John, and he is overwhelmed.

A word of caution here. These days, if we are to believe everything we hear, it seems any number of people have visions of Jesus—and just carry right on doing what they were doing! John MacArthur writes:

A few years ago I had lunch with a very well-known and influential charismatic pastor. He is also a widely read author and a national media figure. This man told me, 'When I'm shaving in the mornings, Jesus comes into the bathroom and puts his arm around me, and we talk.' He paused to measure my reaction, and then he said, 'John, do you believe that?'

'No, I don't,' I replied, 'but what troubles me most is I think you believe it.'

'Why?' he asked. 'Why is it so hard for you to accept the idea that Jesus visits me in a personal way every morning?'

*Does he keep shaving?* I wondered. *Or does he collapse in utter fear and trembling in the presence of the holy, glorified Lord?* When Isaiah saw the Lord on His throne, he said 'woe is me, for I am ruined!' (Isa. 6:5) Peter saw him and fell on his face and said 'Depart from me, for I am a sinful man, O Lord!' (Luke 5:8) I don't believe anyone could keep shaving in the presence of the risen Lord![2]

Nor, I suspect, would the apostle John! John had known the Lord Jesus in the flesh so very well. He was one of the 'inner three'—Peter, James and John—who were present with Jesus sometimes when others of the twelve were excluded. He was the one who reclined closest to Jesus at the last supper (John 13:23) and was even trusted with the care of Mary the mother of Jesus (John 19:26). Yet for all his closeness, even familiarity, the unveiled glory of the Lord Jesus overwhelms him.

The vision is of Jesus in great glory. But when John identifies him, he uses a familiar phrase that expresses the Lord's humanity: he sees one 'like a son of man.' This phrase was perhaps Jesus' own favourite way of referring to himself; it is used around eighty times in the gospels, mostly on Jesus' own lips. But it is more than a phrase that expresses Jesus' humanity; equally, it points to his glory. The Old Testament prophet Daniel had spoken of 'one like a son of man, coming with the clouds of heaven'; he was given authority, glory and sovereign power and all the nations worshipped him (see Daniel 7:13). This is the one John sees; he too is coming with clouds (1:7); he too—as the rest of the Book of Revelation will make clear—is to be worshipped by people of every nation (see, for example, 5:9 and 11:15).

Who, then, is this Lord Jesus who is to be worshipped? Of the four gospels, John's is the clearest in teaching that Jesus is God—see, for example, John 1:1 where John says it, and 20:28, where Thomas admits it and Jesus accepts it. That same high understanding of who Jesus is continues here in Revelation, as we will see several times. Look at verse 17, where Jesus declares himself to be the First and the Last. Then look at verse 8, where the Lord God Almighty declares himself to be the Alpha and Omega. Alpha and Omega are the first and last letters of the Greek alphabet; God is saying he is the First and the Last. In fact, it is unclear in verse 8 whether it is God the Father speaking, or God the Son; and it is unclear because the same things can be said about each. They are equally first and last; they are equally one 'who is, and who was, and who is to come, the Almighty' (verse 8; compare it with verse 4). What God is, Jesus is. So it is no surprise in verse 4 when the benediction ('grace and peace') come from Father, Spirit and Son. After all, there are other similar benedictions in other parts of Scripture (2 Corinthians 13:14 is one famous and obvious example).

Why is the Holy Spirit referred to as 'the seven spirits' or 'the seven-fold Spirit' in verse 4? Perhaps because the letters will be sent to seven churches, and this reminds us that the Spirit is with each one. Or perhaps it echoes Isaiah 11:2, where seven different titles are given to the Holy Spirit. Whatever the reason, it is clear that the Holy Spirit is the Spirit referred to here.

Now take a moment to read this description of Jesus' glory again. No vision can exceed this. Even his feet glow like bronze, like bronze glowing in a furnace. But even the glowing feet are dimmed by comparison with his face, a face which shines like the Sun in all its brilliance. It hurts the eyes to catch even a glimpse of the glory of the Lord Jesus! His voice, too, is like no human voice. It sounds like a torrent of water, full of power. Stars are no longer awesome globes of fire scattered throughout the universe, but things that he can hold in his hand. Those stars, as we will see, represent the angels of the seven churches—seven churches represented by the seven golden lampstands (verses 12, 20). Among those churches walks Jesus, the glorious Lord.

Jesus has come to give John a message for these churches, a message which is to be sent to the 'angel' of each church (see, for example, 1:20 and 2:1).

There has been much discussion about the meaning of 'angel' here. In English, angel has one obvious meaning, but in the original Greek it is an ordinary word meaning 'messenger.' It is likely that these 'messengers' of the churches are their pastors; who else should such letters be sent to? Some suggest that each church has its own guardian angel, and that is the 'angel' referred to here. But why would such a spirit-being be sent a letter? And what would he do with it? The most important point, though, is that these stars/angels are held in the hands of the Lord; they are under his control and must hear his voice. The churches themselves are the lampstands, and

Jesus walks among his churches. He is always present with them; those 'eyes like blazing fire' see what is happening at every point. How important it is to remember this. What a difference it would make, for example, to our leaders' meetings and to our church business meetings if we really believed that the Lord walked among us! Yet he does; even though we cannot see him, he sees us. And he makes it clear in the letters he writes that much that he sees does not please him! Remember those eyes!

If we are going to understand Revelation at all, we must know the Christ who gives it. He himself is its chief focus; before we go on to consider the letters he writes and the people he writes to, therefore, we must consider first the sender of the letters. We must consider the Christ of Revelation.

## 1. He is crowned : 'the ruler of the kings of the earth'

Earth has many kings and great men; they arise, they flourish for a while and then they are gone. At the time of this vision, Emperor Domitian was the most powerful man on the earth. That was something to strike terror into the hearts of Christians, because Domitian was no friend to the gospel. In truth, kings and great men very rarely are. Domitian had shown his hatred of the gospel by exiling many of its messengers; John, in exile on Patmos, was one of them. All down the ages this pattern has been repeated. Governments of whatever kind seem, at best, to tolerate the gospel; often, they seek to destroy it. In our own day, the great Soviet power tried its utmost to destroy the gospel. It failed, but the church there bore a terrible cost. China, too, has seen many Christian martyrs to Communism. Now it seems certain that Islam—which always hates the Jesus of the New Testament—will take up the cudgel against the gospel in many countries. It is not an unusual thing to suffer for the gospel's sake. In fact, Jesus warns the church at Philadelphia that although they might have suffered much so far, a day of far greater evil is coming, and coming on the whole world (3:10).

But the message John brings to these people is a striking reminder that Domitian is not the ruler of earth at all. That honour belongs to Jesus their Lord. He is 'the ruler of the kings of the earth' (verse 5) and 'King of Kings and Lord of Lords' (19:16). Domitian in his day and every ruler since (whether good or tyrannical) has, ultimately, been under the rule of King

Jesus. The Lord Jesus had already said 'all authority in heaven and on earth has been given to me' (Matthew 28:18). It is true now, and it was already true in John's day. We do not need to wait for some distant time when that will become true; Jesus is not some 'king in waiting', frustrated at what is happening and only waiting until he has the power so that he can intervene. He is already King; he is already ruling.

Then why …? We can hear the questions John's first readers might have asked. We can hear them because we too have asked them! If Jesus is King already (and we do not want to doubt it), then why is there so much suffering? Why, in particular, do so many Christians suffer?

Let us be honest: we are not given a complete answer in the Bible at all. But we are given *some* answers. Know this, says the Bible to those who are suffering under the reign of kings: not one king arises, unless Jesus calls him by name. 'By me,' he says, 'Kings rule' (Proverbs 8:15). Jesus' kingship is an eternal kingship; when he said 'My kingdom is not of this world' (John 18:36), he was speaking of its eternity. Though earthly kings reign and die, reign and die, yet Jesus 'shall reign for ever and ever' (11:15).

'But,' one of John's readers might want to cry out, 'Do you not know that we are *dying*? Do you not know that again and again, Lord, your servants are not only suffering for you, but dying for you also?' The church in Pergamum already has its own martyr, Antipas (2:13). Does Jesus know? Of course he does; it is part of his glory that he holds 'the keys of death and Hades' (1:18). No-one can die, no-one can pass into Hades (the place of the dead), unless Jesus first unlocks the door. He himself (of course!) has been dead, and been in Hades (Acts 2:27, 31 in the original Greek). What does Hades mean here?

'It is evident that the term 'Hades' *as used here* cannot mean hell or the grave. It signifies the state of disembodied existence. It refers to the state of death which results when life ceases and when body and soul separate. Thus Hades always follows death (Rev. 6:8).'[3]

God does not anywhere promise that his people will not suffer. Jesus does not offer to keep them from martyrdom. Instead, he comforts them by reminding them that nothing happens to them, nothing at all, without his permission. He is Lord indeed. Not only is he Lord of death and Hades, he is Lord too over all of history. In chapter 5 we will see a scroll, sealed with seven seals. It becomes clear that it is the scroll of history, and no-one can open its seals. John weeps because there is no-one worthy; but he is told 'The lion of the tribe of Judah ... has triumphed. He is able to open the scroll and its seven seals' (5:5). John turns, expecting to see the Lion. Instead, we are given one of the most dramatic contrasts in literature anywhere, as John sees not a Lion, but a Lamb—and the Lamb has been slain. It is Jesus, of course; and the book of Revelation is the Lamb opening the seals, and history unfolding—as we will see.

What else do we need to know about the Lord Jesus if we are to understand Revelation?

## 2. He is crucified

Oddly enough, there is always a danger that Christ's church will forget this. Although the cross is the most common Christian symbol, and although the communion service is a deliberate reminder of the cross, yet it is still true that Christians lose sight far more than we should of the greatest fact of all: our Lord was crucified. We do not *actually* forget, but we may not give its truth the prominence and emphasis that we should. It is all too easy to concentrate on Jesus crowned King so much that we expect unbroken triumph for ourselves and for his church. But the King we serve was once hung in weakness and shame on a Roman gibbet. It is always a mistake to make so much of Christ the King that we forget Christ the crucified.

Why did he come into the world? We know the answer. He came to free us from our sin and our sins by his blood, as this verse says.

Once before, God's people were 'freed by blood.' It happened when Israel was in Egypt, and a Passover lamb had to be sacrificed (Exodus 12). On one dreadful night the angel of the Lord swept through Egypt, and every house that was not marked out by blood experienced a death. But the Hebrews had been warned; they marked their own houses with blood and were spared. But more than that, they were delivered: for that very night Pharaoh commanded them to leave Egypt. They were no longer slaves; they had been freed by blood.

Blood speaks of sacrifice; of a life violently laid down. As Jesus died he paid a redemption price, carrying the guilt of our sin and the punishment we deserve and setting us free. Though once we were far away and alienated from him because of our sinful attitudes and behaviour, he came to make us into the people of God. He came to make us a kingdom of priests (a phrase also used at the time of the Exodus: see Exodus 19:6) to serve God. Out of his great love he endured the cross for us. For the joy set before him (Hebrews 12:2) he went to Calvary. Before the crown came the cross—and so it is for us. Revelation is written to encourage us to believe that though we may have to endure many trials and even be put to death, yet we shall live and reign with him. Again and again we will see this theme as we read and study Revelation.

Revelation is a book about the suffering of God's people, and how they triumph in and through that suffering. Triumph is only possible because of the cross. Sometimes, we are able to see how that works out in the lives of individual Christians. As just one example, a friend of ours became very ill. He was an elderly man and he (and we) were sure that his time on earth was coming to a close. Then—to everyone's surprise—he made a remarkable recovery. Pleased to be well again, grateful for all that God had done, yet he confessed that he was disappointed. Though his illness had been severe and his suffering had been great, he had fully expected to be going home to heaven. He looked forward to it so much that even recovery was a disappointment. It is that kind of triumph that the cross of Christ brings— the only kind of triumph that can stand in the face of death—whenever it comes.

## 3. He is coming

But if Jesus *was* crucified and *is* crowned as king, it is equally certain that he is coming again. Revelation begins and ends with a reference to this great coming; all through the book the tension mounts as we await the day of the Lord's return. It is no exaggeration to say that it is the whole message of Revelation.

'Look, he is coming with the clouds' (1:7). As we have seen, this phrase is very similar to one used by Daniel: 'In my vision at night I looked, and there before me was one like a son of man, coming with the clouds of heaven. He approached the Ancient of Days and was led into his presence' (Daniel 7:13). But there is a difference; Daniel's vision seems to speak of Jesus after his resurrection ascending back into the presence of his Father and receiving (as the man Christ Jesus) all glory and power. John however uses the phrase to speak of the glorious return of Jesus, that time when 'every eye will see him, even those who pierced him; and the peoples of the earth will mourn because of him' (verse 7).

When he comes, every eye will see him. There is no hint of a secret return here; on the contrary, it could not be more public. Even those who pierced him, even those who hated him, will see him. Though John wants us to know that his return will bring great joy for those who have trusted him, it will also mark the beginning of great mourning, for judgement will surely follow.

So John wants to tell us that 'this same Jesus' who died on a cross, rose from the dead and ascended to the right hand of the Father where he reigns over the universe—yes, this same Jesus—is the one who will one day come again. This time he will not 'lay his glory by'. He will not make himself nothing and take the form of a servant (see Philippians 2:7). This time all his glory will come with him, and we shall see him as he is.

As we work through Revelation and its various sections, time and again we will follow a section to its end, expecting that it will end by describing the return of Jesus in glory. But time and again, instead, we will see that the section ends just before his coming, almost—but not quite—at the very point of his return. While the last section of the book, as we shall see, ends *after* the coming of the Lord, each of the others stops just short; it is as if the book is full of delays. For example, at 8:1, just as we expect the seventh seal we get… silence! Similar delays happen at other points; it is John's way of taking us on to another, parallel, section and starting (as it were) the vision again. These repeated delays find an echo in the experience of the church. Time and again in history, everything has seemed to point to the nearness of the Coming. Time and again, servants of Jesus have said with great conviction 'It must be now; surely we are the last generation.' But we are still waiting; 'I am coming soon' plainly did not mean to the Lord what it means to us! But it is not that 'the prophetic clock has stopped'; rather, it is that we await his time.

As we wait, and as we experience something of the suffering that come to all those who will enter the kingdom of God (see Acts 14:22 and 2 Timothy

3:12), we must not despair. Why? Because for us, as for him, the cross is the way to the crown. When we are 'under the cross' the crown follows. Christ was dead, but is alive; and he is the true ruler of the Kings of the earth. Domitian is gone and all but forgotten; Christ reigns still.

See what rich things we are told about our Lord Christ in just a few words, in verses 5–7. We are told of his proclamation ('the faithful witness'), of his resurrection ('the firstborn from the dead'), of his exaltation ('the ruler of the kings of the earth'), of his redemption ('freed us from our sins by his blood'), of his salvation ('made us to be a kingdom and priests to serve his God and Father') and of his consummation ('Look, he is coming with the clouds, and every eye will see him'). Every one of these is precious to the suffering believer. He is the faithful witness—every word of his can be trusted. He is risen from the dead, and death should hold no fear then for us. He is the ruler of the kings of the earth, and no king, however wicked, can do anything to us that our Lord Jesus does not allow. I am certain that you can work out the others for yourself!

Our own day may see trouble for us and trouble for the church. In the western world we may well need—within a few years—the message of Revelation as we have never needed it before. Then we will need to know: he was crucified for us; he defeated death for us; he is crowned for us—and he is coming—for us! What a glory fills our eyes! What a glory fills our souls at the prospect!

**NOTES**

1 Quoted in **Iain Murray,** *The Puritan Hope* (Edinburgh: The Banner of Truth Trust, 1973), pp. 262–263

2 **John MacArthur,** *Charismatic Chaos* (Grand Rapids: Zondervan, 1992) page 37

3 **William Hendriksen,** *More than Conquerors* (Leicester: IVP, 1973), p. 57; emphasis added. For more on Hades, see the same author's *The Bible on the Life Hereafter* (Grand Rapids: Baker Book House, 1959).

# A kingdom and priests

Please read again Revelation chapter 1

In our last chapter we glanced briefly at the Lord Jesus Christ, the great subject of the book of Revelation. In this chapter we must look equally briefly at his people, the people of God. They too play a major part in the book, and they too are introduced in these first verses. They are described as those who have been freed from their sins by the blood of Christ (verse 5), and have been made by him into a kingdom and priests (or a kingdom of priests) to serve God the Father (verse 6). What do we need to know about these people—a people to whom, if we have true faith, we most certainly belong?

## Their identity—not a people

Oddly enough perhaps, the first thing we need to know about them is that they were 'not a people.' In Hosea, God says 'I will say to those called "Not my people", "You are my people" and they will say "You are my God,"' (Hosea 2:23). Earlier, God had said through the same prophet 'In the place where it was said to them "You are not my people" they will be called "sons of the Living God"' (Hosea 1:10). So that we are not in any doubt about what this means, Paul quotes these verses (in Romans 9:25–26) and shows that they refer to all those—Jew and Gentile—who have become God's people through faith in Christ. All national distinctions have gone; now from every nation, tribe and tongue (Revelation 7:9) God has called a people. More than that, he has chosen those he will call: those who are his followers are his *chosen* followers (17:14). Just as God had planned from all eternity that Jesus, the Lamb of God, would be slain—so that he is called 'The Lamb that was slain from the creation of the world' in Revelation 13:8—so God had planned who of all the inhabitants of the world would be saved through Jesus: their names were 'written in the book of life from the creation of the world' (17:8).

These chosen people of God have no visible marks on them to allow us to recognise them in advance; we only know who they are when they come to believe the gospel. We cannot even begin to predict who will respond to the gospel when they hear it. Experience shows that we are very often surprised! Again and again, those who seem to have every advantage reject the gospel; they have godly Christian parents, are taken to good churches with good children's and young people's work, and so on. Yet they reject the truth, and never come to Christ. On the other hand some of the least 'promising candidates'—with lives full of every kind of sin and hearts that seem very hard—hear the good news with joy, respond with gladness and become exemplary saints! John Newton, for example, was an immoral, cruel, foul-mouthed slave trader. He was one of the least likely candidates for a Christian to witness to; and doubtless if any had tried they would have received a tongue-lashing for their pains. Yet God intervened in his life, and made him a Christian and a preacher of remarkable ability and grace. Or nearer to our own day, Nicky Cruz was leader of a New York street gang, violent and apparently careless of what anyone else thought about him. But again, the love of Christ reached him and changed him. Or Doreen Irvine— a prostitute and involved in witchcraft—another 'most unlikely case' for Christ's kingdom. Yet all of these and many, many more were reached, saved and transformed by Christ's love and power.

## Freed from sin

Those who trust Christ belong together, and they have been forgiven. More than that, though, they have been freed from their sins by Christ's blood (verse 5).

Centuries earlier, the Jewish people had lived in bondage in Exodus. God raised up Moses to set them free, but Pharaoh could only be persuaded to let them go after God unleashed a series of terrible plagues on the nation. The last plague sent the angel of death into every house in Egypt to kill the first-born son; only those houses that killed a lamb and sprinkled its blood on their doorposts were exempt. After the devastation of that night, Pharaoh let the people go (see Exodus 12); this is the Passover. In a very real sense, the Jews were set free by blood.

In the New Testament, Christ is the Passover lamb (1 Corinthians 5:7) whose blood sets us free from sin. It does not mean that we never sin again;

it does mean that its power over us is broken. We will never feel the punishment that our sins deserve, and one day our redemption will be complete: in heaven, we will be free from sin in every sense. There is no need for us to feel despair or that we are not converted because we still sin—'if we claim to be without sin, we deceive ourselves' (1 John 1:8). Instead, we confess our sin knowing that the blood of Jesus will cleanse us from it (1 John 1:9), and we look with hope and expectation for the day when we will sin no more.

## The need to hear

But (obviously) no-one can believe the gospel unless they hear the gospel (Romans 10:14), and so the gospel has to be preached to everyone indiscriminately. All creation must hear the good news, (Mark 16:15) as repentance and forgiveness of sins is preached to all nations (Luke 24:47). Have you ever walked down the street on a calm summer evening and caught in the air the tantalising smell of a barbecue? If you are on your way to share in the feast, the smell becomes a foretaste of the food to come. But if you are not invited it is only a reminder of how hungry you are. So it is with the gospel. Some hear it and respond to it: it becomes the promise of life, a down-payment of glory to come. Others hear the same gospel but harden their hearts against it. To them, the same gospel becomes a reminder of their need, and a warning of judgement to come. For those who hear the gospel but never believe it, the gospel and its message are a smell of death (2 Corinthians 2:16). But to others, the gospel is life itself. They hear, they respond, and they become the people of God.

## Their identity: now a people

Secondly, we must notice that those who are saved *become* a people. Salvation is, of course, for individuals. People hear the gospel as individuals, respond to it individually and so become Christians individually. But salvation is not *just* individual, as the Bible makes clear. Those who become Christians are said to belong to a family (Galatians 6:10), the family of God. They are said to be joined together as a building (Ephesians 2:21) where individual stones, perhaps very different from one another (Christians are called living stones, not bricks! Bricks are all the same, but stones are all different), are harmoniously joined together to form one building. Here in our text they are called a kingdom. All these pictures are used to remind us that Christians belong to one another.

There is a very real sense in which it is true to say that outside the church there is no salvation. This phrase has often been mis-used, particularly by the Roman Catholic church. But properly used it is true; only the church of Jesus has the message of salvation, and all those who respond to that message become part of that church. And because they are part of the church—the church of Christ world-wide—they ought also to become part of a local, individual church. While sometimes we meet people who claim to be Christians but never get involved with a local church at all, we must remember that the Lord Jesus himself said 'whatever you did for one of the least of these brothers of mine, you did for me' (Matthew 25:40). In other words, how we react to his church shows us how we really feel about Jesus himself. We cannot say 'Yes' to Jesus but 'No' to his church. Salvation makes us part of the family of God, part of the Kingdom of Jesus.

Kingdoms do have Kings, and it is as King that the Lord Jesus is presented most often in Revelation.

The well-known appeal to the church at Laodicea in 3:20 for example ('I stand at the door and knock. If anyone hears my voice and opens the door, I will come in and eat with him and he with me') is made as a King, for he goes on 'to him who overcomes I will give the right to sit with me on my throne ...' Jesus is certainly offering mercy here, but not as a powerless servant unable to do anything without permission. He is the King! It is as King he offers mercy, and because he is King it is mercy on his terms. He is presented as King, too, in this very first chapter; he is ruler of the Kings of the earth (1:5) that is, the King of Kings and Lord of Lords. Whatever Kings there are in the world, whatever Lords or rulers there might be, Jesus is King over them all. Though they may oppose him and make war against the Lamb of God (and earthly rulers often do), he will triumph over them because he is Lord of Lords and King of Kings (17:14). And when he triumphs, with him are his chosen and faithful followers (same text)—for kingdoms not only have Kings, they have subjects too. Here, the subjects are described as 'priests.'

All Christians are priests. One of the strangest thing in the church over the last few decades has been the seemingly endless debate about women priests: should women be priests, or not? The constant answer of the Bible is: they already are! All Christian women are priests, all Christian men are priests. There are no exceptions, and there is no special class of people within the church called 'priests.' All of us are priests; Jesus is the one High Priest and the sacrifice he made is one sacrifice for all times (Hebrews 7:27). It is rather salutary that the biggest debate in the church over the last few years has been completely irrelevant—but if we believe our Bibles, it has been![1]

## The function of priests

A priest is someone who represents human beings in the presence of God. There are two basic things that a priest—in whatever religion—does; first, he makes sacrifices for the people, and secondly he makes intercession (prays) for them. So as our great priest, Jesus first of all made a sacrifice for us, the sacrifice of his own body once for all (Hebrews 10:10). That one sacrifice is completely sufficient: it never fails, and it never has to be repeated; that's what the apostle means when he says 'we have been made holy through the sacrifice of the body of Jesus once for all.' God himself was involved in the sacrifice: 'God presented [Jesus] as a sacrifice of atonement' (Romans 3:25) therefore it can never fail. It is because the Lord Jesus is the sacrifice, as well as the priest who makes the sacrifice, that Revelation pictures him 'dressed in a robe dipped in blood, (19:13).

But secondly, as our great priest Jesus prays for us: ' he is able to save completely those who come to God through him because he always lives to intercede for them' (Hebrews 7:25). As our ever-living Saviour, there are three parts to his work. First, he himself appears in heaven on our behalf. Second, he appears there as the one who died for our pardon, a death that gives both life and power to his intercession for us. Third, in the presence of God he continues to make known to the Father his great desires for his church, for his bride. As he prayed for us in John 17, so those great prayers continue to be offered by him. It is not, though, that he needs to keep repeating those prayers. It is very likely that no words are necessary; his presence before God's throne is enough. Just as God tells us that he set the rainbow in the heavens to remind *him* (not Noah) of his covenant with Noah, so the presence of Jesus in heaven is a constant reminder to God—

who can never forget!—to work all things together for the good of those that love him (Romans 8:28).

But our text does not speak of Jesus as priest, but rather of all his people being a kingdom of priests, royal priests. One part of a priest's work, as we have seen, is prayer; that is easy enough to understand. But what are our sacrifices? If the sacrifice of Jesus was once and for all, sufficient for all time (and it was), then it is easy enough to say what our sacrifices are not; they are not atoning. They do not contribute to our salvation; that price has been paid already. What then are they? Peter describes them as spiritual sacrifices (1 Peter 2:5)—that is, they are not physical animals—and they include at least the following:

First, the sacrifice of praise (Hebrews 13:15). God would no longer be pleased if we were to sacrifice bulls and goats, but he is pleased—delighted, in fact—when we sing his praise, or when we talk to one another about his greatness, building one another up as well as bringing glory to him. This is a sacrifice we should be offering continually.

Second, the sacrifice of lives lived in obedience to him. 'Offer your bodies as living sacrifices, holy and pleasing to God—this is your spiritual act of worship' (Romans 12:1). All of us have to admit that we have spent more than enough time in the past doing what pagans do—'living in debauchery, lust, drunkenness, orgies, carousing and detestable idolatry' (1 Peter 4:3). Now our unconverted friends think it strange—and they think us strange—that we no longer join in with them; but it is our duty and privilege now to use our bodies in different ways, in ways that serve and honour God rather than dishonouring him. With such sacrifices, God is well pleased.

Third, the use of our money to support God's work. When Paul wrote to the Philippians he praised them for sharing in his troubles, especially by supporting him and others financially. Sadly, only they had done this ('not one church shared with me in the matter of giving and receiving, except you only,' he writes (Philippians 4:15). But their gifts have been priestly offerings, 'an acceptable sacrifice, pleasing to God' (4:18). And though God is delighted with their gifts, yet he will not let them outgive him; so Paul promises them 'my God will meet all your needs according to his glorious riches in Christ Jesus' (4:19).

These are our sacrifices, our offerings to God. They are acceptable when made through Christ Jesus (1 Peter 2:5); without him, we can do nothing that pleases God. But in the name of our great High Priest, we all have become priests who minister to God and bring him delight.

We are not just priests, however—we are kings and priests, or royal priests. In the Old Testament, no-one could be both a king and a priest. One king, Uzziah, tried to offer sacrifices and so make himself a priest (2 Chronicles 26:16–21) and was destroyed by God for it. But God had wanted the whole nation not just to be a holy nation, but to be a kingdom of priests (Exodus 19:6). Now, in Christ, that desire is fulfilled. All God's people are priests; and all God's people are royal, for they have been adopted into the family of God himself.

If God has on earth a special group of people who are his royal priests, we would expect them to be recognised and exalted in the world. But we would also have expected that if God himself came into the world he would bring glory with him and everybody would know who he was. Such expectations would be wrong! We know that when the Son of God came, few recognised him, many hated him and in the end a whole nation agreed to his murder. It is to be no different for God's own people, this royal priesthood to whom Revelation is addressed.

John himself is suffering for his faith. By this time, it is virtually certain that all the other apostles were dead; some of them had died as martyrs. John by contrast is a living martyr, exiled on the island of Patmos 'because of the word of God and the testimony of Jesus' (1:9). But he is not the only one to suffer for Christ; it is in fact the normal Christian life. So he describes himself in the same verse as 'your brother and companion in the suffering and kingdom and patient endurance that are ours in Jesus'. Suffering is ours in Jesus. It is what we are destined for. We are destined for death (Hebrews 9:27) and after that destined for glory (1 Corinthians 2:7). But before either death or glory, we are destined for trials (1 Thessalonians 3:3). He goes on (in effect) to say 'When we were with you we kept telling you that we would be persecuted, and now I'm writing to you to remind you of that, so that these trials do not unsettle you' (see verse 4).

And that, too, is what the book of Revelation is for. Many of its first readers had already known much trouble—afflictions, poverty, even martyrdoms. More was still to come. John writes later of the Great Tribulation (7:14). Some Christians see this as a particular time of trial just before the end. Others—without denying that there are times when the suffering is worse than at others (2:10) see it rather as describing 'the awesome totality of tribulation which from century to century has been the experience of the people of God'.[2] Either way, suffering is to be expected; Jesus himself said 'No servant is greater than his Master. If they persecuted me, they will persecute you also' (John 15.20).

In the Western world, we have known virtually no persecution for generations. We may have to endure a little teasing, perhaps; or we may feel our testimony makes us unpopular and leads to us being passed over for promotion. For most of us that is about as bad as it gets. But there are signs that this situation may not last much longer, even in the UK. As I write, the Independent Television Commission has recently chosen to fine the 'Dream Family Network' (formerly the 'God Channel') £20,000 for screening an advert that 'claimed that Jesus said that he is the only way to salvation, and that homosexual practice is against Biblical teaching.' The ITC said that these views were 'not fit for broadcast.'[3] Without wanting to be alarmist, this and other similar stories may be the first clouds bringing a storm of trouble for the church of Christ. It will be nothing new; it is what we are destined for.

There are only two options at such a time: we may 'soft-pedal' more and more things that the world finds unpopular, until at last we have nothing at all left to say. Or we must be willing to bear witness to unpopular truths, and call the sinful and disobedient to repentance and salvation. The second option is the Biblical one! It is the way that Jesus went, and the way his disciples must follow. But when we do, we must be prepared to take whatever such faithfulness brings. It is a theme we will return to again and again in Revelation. For example, in 2:10 the Lord tells the church at Smyrna that they need to be faithful 'even to the point of death.' Peter told his readers 'to this you were called, because Christ suffered for you, leaving you an example, that you should follow in his steps' (1 Peter 2:21). Maybe even at this moment you are suffering in some degree because you are a Christian. It might be that you are mocked and teased—perhaps even bullied—at school because of your faith. Or perhaps you are a preacher, facing trouble in your church because of the truths you love and proclaim. Or maybe you work for a large company and cannot get promotion because you refuse to adopt worldly attitudes to sin and tolerance. Or you may be from a Muslim or Jewish family, cast out—and even under threat—because of your faith in Jesus. None of these things should surprise us.

There is only one way to be faithful; it is to remember who is really in control. So John has already told them (as the Lord Jesus told him) that Jesus holds the keys of death (1:18). No-one ever passes through the door of death until the Lord Jesus has unlocked it for them. John will go on to assure his readers, and us, of ultimate victory: many will come who 'will make war against the Lamb, but the Lamb will overcome them because he is Lord of lords and King of kings—and with him will be his called, chosen and faithful followers' (17:14). This kingdom of priests, who will be faithful to the end, will in the end reign on the earth (5:10)—that is, the new earth, remade by Christ himself as a place where righteousness is at home (2 Peter 3:13). In that new creation, the people of God will reign with their God for ever and ever with no more crying or tears or suffering. These things belong to the old order, and the old order has passed away, gone for ever. This is what it is to belong to the people of God; it is to be prepared to suffer for a little while, and to be looking forward to reigning, knowing that suffering *is* but for a little while, but reigning is for ever.

**Notes**

**1** The question of whether women should teach and lead the church, however, is not irrelevant. For a full discussion, see **John Piper and Wayne A. Grudem (eds),** *Recovering Biblical Manhood and Womanhood* (Wheaton: Crossway Books, 1991) or **Brian Edwards (ed.),** *Men, women and authority* (Epsom: DayOne,1996)

**2** **P. E. Hughes,** *The Book of the Revelation* (Leicester: IVP, 1990).

**3** Reported in *Evangelicals Now* (February 2000).

# What the Lord Christ hates in his church

Please read Revelation chapters 2 & 3

A pastor died and went to heaven. There was not much of a queue before the Great Throne—this is heaven, after all—and he joined himself to the end of the few that were waiting. He was pretty confident. He knew he was a sinner of course; but he knew he was a saved sinner and was confident that his work would stand examination. His church had worked hard under his leadership, and as a consequence had grown considerably. They had developed many different ministries and outreaches and even begun their own Bible school. When it was necessary, they had disciplined those who persisted in sin, and done everything they could to maintain the purity of the church. They had quite a reputation for their warning ministry too; false apostles and prophets and teachers had arisen and they had always been dealt with speedily and thoroughly. The reputation of his church was world-wide; anybody visiting their city was likely to be told: this was The Church to go to.

As the pastor joined the short queue, he saw one or two people in front that he recognised. They had not belonged to churches as sound as his, but he still was not in the least surprised to see them here. But what a good job for them, he thought to himself, that salvation is all grace! He watched as they were welcomed, and raised his eyebrows in surprise at their rewards. He believed in rewards, of course; one of his best known sermons was titled 'On the judgement of rewards and its relevance to the sovereign, free grace of God.' But, to be honest, he was more than a little surprised that these folks whose churches had seemed to be all hay and stubble had received a reward at all. Well, that's grace for you. He was confident when it was his turn; he actually found himself humming 'Bold I approach the eternal throne' as he walked up to the throne.

The voice of Jesus was awesome. Even 'a sound like many waters' simply did not begin to describe it. He was so struck by the voice itself that at first he barely took in what Jesus was saying. 'You are welcome here, my brother,' said the awesome Voice, 'Welcome to the kingdom prepared for you from the beginning of the world. But I have no reward for you.'

The pastor was dumbfounded. 'No reward?' he spluttered. 'But look at my church; look at what we've done; look at all the ministries and the missionaries and the meetings…' (Strange how much of a habit alliteration had become!) The Voice smiled sadly. 'Yes,' the pastor heard it say, 'But you had left your love for me far behind! All those things you did—none of them sprang from love. There were different motives governing your actions.'

'Left our love for you, Lord? But you were what it was all about. You were there, all the time—weren't you?'

'Oh, yes,' said the Voice, 'I was there. But I was on the outside—and though I knocked many times, no-one ever came to let me in.'

That pastor could have been from the church at Ephesus which had been noted for its discrimination and hard work (2:2). He could have been from Sardis (which certainly had a reputation [3:1]). Or he could have been from Laodicea, which somehow managed to keep its Lord on the outside (3:20).

## Seven churches, seven letters

Seven churches have a letter sent to them by the Lord of glory; seven churches hear what he thinks about them. How would you feel if it were your church? The 'angel' of the churches (2:1,8,12,18 and 3:1,7,14) might refer to their pastors—the word 'angel' is from the ordinary Greek word for a messenger. If your pastor stood up next Sunday and was able to say he had a personal letter from the Lord Jesus—written to and about your own church—how would you feel? Would you be joyous, happy, confident? Most churches, I fear—perhaps even yours and mine—would be in for stern talk and severe warnings. I say that not because I am a natural pessimist, nor because I know anything in particular about your church. Rather, it is because that is (for the most part) what the Lord Christ did for these churches in Revelation. For the most part, I say; of Smyrna and Philadelphia he makes no criticism (what a relief it must have been for them! And what blessed churches to belong to!). But of Laodicea, by contrast, he has nothing good to say at all.

# Chapter 3

In these chapters we will not look at each church individually. Instead, we will look at all the churches together and see first what the Lord Jesus hates in his churches. Then, in the next chapter we will see what he loves in his churches, trying to learn lessons from both. So, what does Christ hate in his churches?

## Lack of love

Christ's letter to the Ephesians (Rev. 2:1–7) may well describe perfectly many churches today. Some churches in our own day seem to have lost all sense of truth; while they may believe and preach the Bible themselves, they see nothing wrong in fellowship with all kinds of churches and individuals who believe the exact opposite to themselves. They do it in the name of love and humility: no group, they say, has a monopoly on truth. If someone says they follow Jesus, who are we to quibble? Thankfully, there are many churches who can see through that kind of approach. They know that there is such a thing as 'the faith that was once for all entrusted to the saints' (Jude 3) that has to be contended for. They do not get involved in argument for the sake of it, but neither can they compromise by 'fellowship' with those who, for example, deny the Scriptures, or the deity of Christ, or justification by faith. They know that to do so is not love or humility, but unfaithfulness! The church at Ephesus was just like that; they were hard working, persevering, disciplining ('cannot tolerate wicked men') and discriminating ('tested those who claim to be apostles but are not'). But they had a problem that was so big that their virtues barely counted; they were lacking in love for Jesus.

A wrong use of doctrine so often produces people and churches like this; we love soundness, we love the fact that we are not carried away by the excesses of others, we love our standards and our work; but we have left our love for the Lord.

Please note that it does say 'left'; it is often misquoted as 'you have *lost* your first love'—but that would be an accident. The Lord says 'You have *forsaken* your first love'—and that's deliberate. Somehow, in the midst of their Christian lives, in the midst of all their hard work, in the midst of doing so many things that are good and right, they had begun to do them for the wrong reason. It was no longer love for the Lord Jesus that motivated them; love had been left far behind.

It is not possible to love the Lord Jesus without living the right kind of life; Jesus himself said 'If you love me you will obey what I command' (John 14:15). But it is all too easy to do the right things for wrong motives; to keep up the motions of being a Christian and of church life and let our busy-ness and the rightness of our actions disguise the fact that we no longer love Jesus as we did.

## Tolerance

The Lord Jesus Christ hates tolerance! But what a shocking idea that would be to many people, even people who regard Jesus as a great religious teacher. Tolerance seems to be one of the most popular gods of the age.

For example, I recently heard a well-known rabbi taking part in a radio discussion programme with a number of other people. He was obviously regarded by his not-very-religious fellows as a good chap. He was liked, listened to and laughed with. What made him so popular? Partly no doubt it was his temperament; he seems to be a jolly fellow with a twinkling, laughing personality. But a large part of his popularity, I am convinced, comes from his tolerance. A Jew himself, he makes no judgement on other people or other religions. I heard him say 'This is true for me,'—but go on to imply that other things, even contradictory things, might be true for other people. Hence his popularity; tolerance is the god of the age. But it is a false god, and Jesus hates it.

We need to turn aside for a little while from the book of Revelation and demonstrate that this is true. Take, for example, the way Jesus speaks of (and to) the Pharisees in Matthew 23. They are, he says, guilty of some spectacular errors. Because they say that an oath taken on the temple means nothing, but an oath taken on the gold of the temple is binding (verse 16) they are fools. It is not a difference of opinion; he does not suggest 'Well, that is true for you, but for me all oaths are binding.' Instead, he calls them hypocrites and blind fools. Because they do many such things, they are like whitewashed tombs, he says (verse 27). Whitewashed tombs—beautiful on the outside but on the inside full of dead men's bones. Stripping away the picture, he says to them 'On the outside you appear to people as righteous but on the inside you are full of hypocrisy and wickedness' (verse 28). There is no suggestion that these Pharisees have interesting insights, or that their beliefs and values may be valid for them but not for others. Most alarming of all to an age of tolerance, he warns them that they will not enter the kingdom of heaven, that those who follow them will not enter the kingdom of heaven, and that they and their followers are sons of hell (verses 13,15)!

On another occasion, Jesus speaks to a Samaritan woman (John 4). She recognises his authority and tries to draw him on one of the great religious questions of the day: where should God be worshipped? Is it, as Jews insisted, only in Jerusalem? Or do the Samaritans have a valid insight when they argue that worship is equally acceptable to God from a mountain in Samaria (verse 20)? Here is a perfect opportunity for Jesus to present his tolerance credentials! But in fact he does not: he first tells her that the whole debate is now irrelevant (because the presence of the Messiah begins a whole new age, verse 21) but then insists too that the Jews are the only source of salvation (verse 22).

Again and again in the four gospels Jesus presents himself as the unique authority: 'You have heard that it was said … but I tell you …' (see Matthew 5:21, 27, 31–33). Jesus claims to have the definitive answer, always. So at the end of Matthew's gospel he commands that the gospel should be preached throughout the world, disciples made of all nations, and that they must be taught 'to obey everything I have commanded you' (28:16–20). In fact, so serious is this whole matter that Jesus himself will decide who enters heaven in the end and who does not (Matthew 7:21–23). When the apostle Paul pronounced a curse on those who taught another gospel (Galatians 1:8–9) he was merely following in his Master's footsteps.

So, now that the point is made, there are two things in particular that we are not to be tolerant of: false doctrine and sinful behaviour. But they are both rampant in some churches.

Before we go any further, though, one important distinction does need to be made. A careful reading of the gospels will show that Jesus loved sinners, and was patient with them always. But his worst fury was reserved always for the religious hypocrites, men he called 'whitewashed tombs' and 'children of hell' (see Matthew 23:27 and 23:15). It must be the same in our churches: we are to be endlessly patient with the sinner, regarding no-one as beyond hope or the love of God. But we are not to tolerate open sin in those who claim to be God's children. This is what the apostle Paul taught when he wrote 'I have written to you in my letter not to associate with sexually immoral people—not at all meaning the people of this world who are immoral, or the greedy and swindlers, or idolaters. In that case you would have to leave this world. But now I am writing to you that you must not associate with anyone who calls himself a brother but is sexually immoral or greedy, an idolater or a slanderer, a drunkard or a swindler. With such a man do not even eat' (1 Corinthians 5:9–11). This distinction is vital, in the name of Christian love, faithfulness to Christ and church purity.

The church at Pergamum had those who held to the teaching of Balaam, as well as some who held to the teaching of the Nicolaitans; the church at Thyatira had a prophetess (dubbed 'Jezebel') whose teaching was false. We do not know what particular errors the Lord has in mind, and that he designates as 'the teaching of Balaam'. Nor do we know anything about the prophecies of Jezebel. The commentaries would no doubt be a great help— if they did not contradict one another quite so much. But what we do know about these errors is that they led to moral laxity. The teaching of Balaam 'taught Balak to entice the Israelites to sin by eating food sacrificed to idols and by committing sexual immorality' (2:14). Jezebel 'misleads my servants into sexual immorality' as well as eating food offered to idols (verse 20).

Once again we live in days of great moral laxity. All around us are temptations to sin. Immorality is rife, and gloried in. If we choose to own no TV we are confronted still by images of perversion even on public billboards. Our own sinful natures are easily captured; even God's servants may be misled into sexual immorality. Worse still, it is tempting to try and find 'good' reasons to do what our sinful natures want. Worse yet, there are many religious teachers who are quite ready to pander to that. We must beware of any doctrine which lowers the standards of Christian behaviour! Beware particularly of any compromise with false religion (represented by 'eating food sacrificed to idols'), and of even the suggestion of sexual immorality (2:14–15,20).

There will be few readers who feel themselves to be without guilt, particularly in the area of sexual morality. Thank God, it is still true that 'the blood of Jesus, [God's] Son, purifies us from all sin' (1 John 1:7). Always, if we confess our sin and turn from it, there is mercy for us. God delights to show mercy. But there is a difference between falling and repenting on the one hand, and choosing to live in the way of sin on the other. The latter is changing 'the grace of our God into a licence for immorality, and [denying] Jesus Christ our only Sovereign and Lord' (Jude 4). There is no salvation for those who live like that, unless they repent. 'Do not be deceived: Neither the sexually immoral nor idolaters nor adulterers nor male prostitutes nor homosexual offenders nor thieves nor the greedy nor drunkards nor slanderers nor swindlers will inherit the kingdom of God' (1 Corinthians 6:9–10). The Lord Jesus hates sin, and died to free us from it; there is no excuse for tolerating it in his church.

## Sleepiness

While Smyrna and Philadelphia are the churches to belong to, Sardis *seems* to be the church to belong to; it has a reputation for life! (3:1) But our Lord is still the one who 'does not look at the things mans looks at' (1 Samuel 16:7) and is never taken in by mere reputation. He reveals here that Sardis is, in fact, asleep, and about to die in its sleep. The problem seems to be that it is not a *working* church; its deeds are 'not complete in the sight of my God.' Do note: a church that has a reputation to be alive may be dying; churches are meant to be working, not sleeping.

Not all work has a point of course. The great Welsh preacher Martyn Lloyd-Jones had a story that he sometimes told. When he was a boy a barn in the area caught fire, and people were running around frantically trying to deal with the situation. In the midst of the barn the local blacksmith was swinging his great, heavy hammer at a central iron post, his muscles rippling with the effort and glowing with the sweat and reflected flames. When someone asked what he was doing he said, 'I just felt I had to do something.' Some activity is pointless; but we must not infer from that that all activity is pointless, nor make an excuse for our own laziness. If our church does not take careful stock of the times and of the area where it is placed, and then do something to meet the people's need of the gospel, then it will come under condemnation, like Sardis. And if our church *is* working, but *we* are not playing our part, then we too will be judged. God has gifted every member of his church for the common good, as Paul says: 'Now to each one the manifestation of the Spirit is given for the common good'

(1 Corinthians 12:7). Some gifts are dramatic 'up front' gifts—of leadership, perhaps, or public speaking, or of evangelism. Some gifts are less dramatic and often less obvious—but still vital: the gift of administration, the gift of hospitality or of a sympathetic ear. What is important is that God has made us what we are, given us the gifts we have and wants us to use them to extend his kingdom and to serve others.

## Indifference

Finally, and worst of all, there is the church in Laodicea. The Lord does not have a single word of commendation for this church. Instead, here we have a church, a true church (called so by the Lord Jesus Christ) which makes him sick. The word, translated so politely in the NIV of 3:16 as 'spit', is the word from which we get 'emetic'—something that causes vomiting.

It is, to say the least, an unlovely picture. It is a disturbing one, too. What is the serious problem that provokes such a strong reaction from the Lord Jesus? It is religious indifference; lukewarmness: 'you are lukewarm—neither hot nor cold' (verse 16).

Laodicea's position on an important trade route made it a very wealthy place, a true 'city of millionaires.' It was so wealthy and self-sufficient that when an earthquake devastated the area in AD 60, Laodicea refused imperial help to rebuild. They were rich, and needed aid from no-one; see verse 17. But the Lord has a quite different opinion of them: wretched, pitiful, poor, blind and naked. This would be a hard judgement for them to take. Not only did they regard themselves as wealthy, they were famous for the manufacture of a type of eye ointment, yet Jesus calls them blind as well as poor. And lukewarm? They would well understand that. Just across the river at Hierapolis water flowed from hot springs, and an impressive irrigation system carried the water to Laodicea. But by the time the water arrived, it was lime-laden, lukewarm and sickly.

How hard spiritual lukewarmness is to deal with! Some people are spiritually cold; they are not interested in spiritual things. But, with patience and the gracious Spirit, they may have their eyes opened and respond with gladness to the truth. Some people on the other hand are warm, sincere, genuine Christian believers. No doubt they still have many faults, but they are pressing on to serve the Lord. What a joy they are! But there is a third group of believers—let us call them that—who are lukewarm. They will agree with everything you say (but nothing matters); they will admit that they are not perfect (but feel they are all right really: 'I am rich; I do not need a thing'). They will even admit to their own lukewarmness, but will not do anything about it. In my own pastoral experience I have seen many of the spiritually cold 'warm up' to Christ and I have had the joy of working with many truly warm Christians. But I have known all too many that are lukewarm and I do not think I have seen even one of them change. To such people Christ says (and I am paraphrasing a little to bring out the force) 'I am about—yes, ready even at this moment— to spew you out of my mouth' (3:16). But first he gives them one last warning; there is still a chance for them. The Jesus who died and lives for ever is always a gracious Saviour; and if they will repent, he will pardon them. He is close; he is at the door and knocking; and oh! what blessings he promises to those who will hear and open the door. First, 'I will come in and eat with him, and he with me,' he says. That is, they will know the joy of renewed communion with the Lord himself as they serve him here below. And then, 'to him that overcomes I will give the right to sit with me on my throne'; that is, after a life-time of joyful fellowship with Christ, they will join him in heaven and continue that fellowship unbroken for ever.

Why should a lukewarm Christian be reading this book? I do not know; but perhaps one will, and perhaps you are that one. Be sure that the Lord knows all about you. Read again his forthright opinion of you in verse 16: 'I am about to vomit you out of my mouth.' Realise how serious this is—and then turn again to his promises in verse 20 and 21: 'Here I am! I stand at the door and knock. If anyone hears my voice and opens the door, I will come in and eat with him, and he with me.' He rebukes you because he loves you and wants you to repent (verse 19); even now there is an opportunity. Will you take it?

'He who has an ear, let him hear what the Spirit says to the churches.'

# What the Lord Christ loves in his church

Please read Revelation 2 and 3

I love getting letters. I'm one of those who fights to be at the door first, who sulks if someone beats me, and who prefers even bills to no post at all. (You don't believe that last one? Well, perhaps I will admit to a slight exaggeration!) But I would not be comfortable at the idea of receiving a letter from the Lord Jesus Christ. I know that he is the One Who Sees—that is one of the names given to God in the Old Testament (Genesis 16:13). Here in these letters to the churches in Revelation, the Lord Jesus Christ reveals that he is still the God who sees—and in particular, one who sees everything about our church life, whether good, bad or indifferent. Before you read any further, reflect on that with particular thought about your church (and your part in that church) in the last month. Would you be any more comfortable than I, at the thought of a letter from the King?

Yet of course, since it is our desire to please him (it is!) such a letter would be a considerable help. He could solve our disputes; he could tell us whether to have organs or guitars, old songs or new, both or neither; he could put old Mrs So-and So in her place—she might possibly take it from him. (Although I have to say I know her quite well, and I'm not convinced that she would.) But he would not do these things; he would focus on major issues; and (I fear) he would warn us severely. We have seen some of those warnings and rebukes in our last chapter. In this chapter we will look at the positive side. In all but one of the churches (Laodicea) the Lord Jesus finds things that are commendable; we will try to find out then what it is that pleases our Lord. Then we will close by looking a little more at Smyrna and Philadelphia, the two churches where the Lord Jesus finds nothing to criticise.

## What Jesus loves in his churches

We might expect—and of course we would be right—that if Jesus hates

one thing, he loves its reverse; so that, since he criticises Ephesus for its lack
of love for him, he loves those churches who have not left their first love.
However, let us focus on some of the things he singles out for attention:

## DEEDS

'I know your deeds, your hard work and your perseverance' he says to
Ephesus. 'I know your deeds, your love and faith, your service and
perseverance, and that you are now doing *more than you did at first*' he says
to Thyatira.

This seems to me to strike a death-blow at that theory of church work
which assumes that all we do is meet on Sunday and pray for revival in the
mid-week. What do such folks think the Lord is commending Thyatira
for—more prayer meetings?

So then, he expects his churches to be working churches; he commends
churches who, far from being complacent, learn to work harder! Perhaps
the church at Thyatira had grown in numbers, so it now had more
'departments'; more ways of doing evangelism, more ways of caring for
one another, more ways of influencing the community.

It is so easy to get complacent: to have a reputation for being alive, to be
satisfied with that. But it is a church's duty, not only to be a working church,
but to be constantly assessing that work: does it still meet the needs? Is there
more we should be doing? Are there areas where our work is being
duplicated unnecessarily—where we could free resources for other areas,
other work which is not being done.

The Scriptures speak of 'good purposes' and of 'act[s] prompted by …
faith' (2 Thessalonians 1:11). Every church should have a program
(whether written down or not) of such good purposes and acts. We are only
limited by our imagination; sadly, that is a very great limitation!

## DISCRIMINATION

There is, as I have suggested, a wrong kind of tolerance; though you would
never know it from looking at much of the church today! Wicked men were
around in Ephesus, who claimed to be apostles but were not. So what? does
it matter? Does anybody care? Yes, it matters a great deal—for apostles
were the mouthpieces of God. They were recognised as the ones entrusted

with revelation; they had authority in the churches, the authority of Christ himself. (That is where the New Testament gets its authority: each of the twenty-seven books was either written by an apostle or with the obvious supervision of an apostle, and so each book has the authority of Christ himself behind it). So the church in Ephesus is commended (2:2) for having tested and rejected the claims of false apostles.

Today, we must deny all claims to authority that are not the Scriptures: whether human reason, church tradition or ongoing revelation. It is not unloving to test these claims and find them wanting; it is an inevitable part of our Christian faith. If we want to please the King, we must learn to be discriminating. If anything at all is clear in the gospels, it is that Jesus accepted the authority of written Scripture. He rebuked the unbelief of the Sadducees, who were the 'liberals' of his day, only accepting things in Scripture that seemed to them to be rational. (Like today's liberals, they found themselves with very little of Scripture left, and even that they seemed to have doubts about.) When they mocked the resurrection of the dead, the Lord Jesus replied 'You are in error because you do not know the Scriptures or the power of God' (Matthew 22:29). When he confronted the Pharisees, who put human tradition above Scripture, he said 'You have a fine way of setting aside the commands of God in order to observe your own traditions! For Moses said, "Honour your father and your mother," and, "Anyone who curses his father or mother must be put to death." But you say that if a man says to his father or mother: "Whatever help you might otherwise have received from me is Corban" (that is, a gift devoted to God), then you no longer let him do anything for his father or mother. Thus you nullify the word of God by your tradition that you have handed down. And you do many things like that' (Mark 7:9–13). The Pharisees were very different from the Sadducees; the Pharisees believed that the Old Testament was the word of God. But if it was uncomfortable—and it often was—they found ways around it. As Jesus said, nullifying the word of God by their tradition. The same error is still around today, in small things and in big things. But a good church will work hard to make sure it obeys, rather than sets aside, the Scriptures. Discrimination is important. Only in that way can we gain the approval of the Lord Jesus.

**DOGGED FAITHFULNESS**

Each church that is commended is, in one form or another, commended for its perseverance (see, for example, Ephesus in 2:2 and Pergamum in 2:13). Sometimes, that perseverance has been sorely tried: Pergamum has seen martyrdom, and yet still holds fast; Satan himself seems to have his throne there, and yet nothing daunts these Christian believers.

It is one thing to start well; we must persevere. It is he who endures to the end who shall be saved. 'You did run well; what has hindered you?' asks Paul of the Galatians. It is not how many baptisms we see, but how many disciples grow; it is not the size of the congregation, but how many persevere.

There are many barriers to such perseverance: there are trials of suffering, there are trials of sin within, there are trials of just keeping on keeping on; but we must persevere.

The Lord Jesus is the great example here; he left heaven's throne; he did not turn back; he persevered through the suffering of the cross into the glory that awaited him. He himself was doggedly faithful, and he gives us strength—if we will but ask—to be doggedly faithful for him. Christ loves dogged faithfulness!

## Learning from Smyrna and Philadelphia

'Don't look for a perfect church,' they say, 'because if you find one and join it, you'll spoil it!' And that's true enough; neither Smyrna nor Philadelphia are perfect. Some people take the advice far too seriously; I suppose every large town has them. I think of one couple with a reputation for moving from one church to another, staying just long enough to discover its faults, real or imagined. They seem, in so many respects, to be very good Christians; though frankly, it's hard to tell. No pastor gets to know them well enough before they are off! From what I know of this particular couple (and they have never been a part of my church), they would not have stayed long in Smyrna or Philadelphia; the Lord Jesus might have been pleased with those churches, but they would not be good enough for his servants!

Smyrna and Philadelphia are churches where the all-seeing eye of Jesus finds nothing to complain about. In church life, as in personal life, the fact that 'we cannot be perfect' can soon become an excuse: 'why bother? Why try? We'll not make it'—and allow all kinds of sin then to prosper.

So the *first lesson to learn* is: it is possible to be a good church! And therefore, it is our duty to be reforming, measuring ourselves by the Scriptures; listening to God speaking to us. It is not our duty to think 'We've made it'—the church that thought that was Laodicea! We must be a changing church—not change for the sake of it, but change to make ourselves more useful to Christ, more conformed to his word.

*Second*, we must learn that being a church that pleases Jesus will not exempt us from suffering. He has to say to the church at Smyrna, 'Do not be afraid of what you are about to suffer.' Job was a godly man and yet suffered; Smyrna was a godly church, and yet suffered. The devil is always active among those who please God (2:10)—but his activity is confined to 'a little while'. Whether the ten days of 2:10 are literal or symbolic hardly matters now, two thousand years later. What matters is that their suffering was only for a little time, but their reward, the crown of life, would be eternal. 'In this world you will have trouble; but take heart; I have overcome the world.'

*Third*, we must learn that being a church that pleases Jesus will not make us popular in the world—not even in the religious world. Both Smyrna and Philadelphia were afflicted with 'the synagogue of Satan—those who claim to be Jews but are not' (2:9, 3:9). In Smyrna they are described as slanderers; in Philadelphia as liars—so that it seems they were causing trouble for the church. Who were they? Probably they were the Jews who had rejected Christ. The New Testament tells us that the true Jew, the 'Israel of God', is the church of the Lord Jesus Christ (Galatians 6:16); the true children of Abraham are those who have Abraham's faith in Abraham's Christ. But the day is coming when these false worshippers will be obliged to confess that Christ has loved those churches. The world that rejects us now, will then have to admit the same.

'I am coming soon,' says the Lord. Hang on in there; you will not be hurt by the second death (3:11)—you will have to die as men call death, but the judgement that follows, and the casting into the lake of fire, is not for you. Instead, you will have a crown; you will be a pillar in the temple of God. There will be intimate communion between Jesus and every saint who perseveres, (3:12). Just a little while, and he who is coming will come; and we will see him, and be changed by beholding him.

He who has an ear, let him hear what the Spirit says to the churches.

# The Lamb on the throne

Please read Revelation chapters 4 & 5

The apostle John is in exile on the island of Patmos. Patmos could best be described as a first century concentration camp, and he is there because of his faith in Christ. It is the Lord's Day—it is Sunday—and somehow he has found refuge from the burdens of that camp to spend some time in worshipping God. He tells us that he is in the Spirit on the Lord's Day, and he begins to hear the voice of his Saviour and his Master. With John, we have seen seven lampstands, and that those lampstands represent seven churches; and we have read the seven letters that the Lord Jesus sends to those churches. We noticed that there is much commendation in the letters, and much criticism too; for many of the churches—though still very young—have turned away from their first love. They have begun to toy with worldliness and immorality and heresy. Yet some of those churches are knowing real persecution and still standing firm, and they are commended for it. The Lord Jesus has eyes of fire; and those eyes reveal to him both the faults and the graces of his churches.

Now in chapter 4 we move into a new section. In fact, chapters 4–7 are one section; you might like to read them all together. This section does not have seven lampstands, but seven seals, and we must look at the opening of those seals. We will split the section into two for our convenience, and just look at chapters four and five in this chapter. Let us begin in chapter 4.

## The throne

The voice of Jesus calls John through a door that he sees standing open in heaven. We know it is the voice of Jesus because he tells us that it is the voice he heard first, the voice like a trumpet—which we can relate back to chapter one. There, you remember, he heard a voice like a trumpet, turned to see it and saw 'one like a Son of Man.' There too (1:12–18) the glory of Jesus is described. Now Jesus calls John to come through this door—in vision, not in reality—into heaven itself, so that he might see what must soon take place.

As he goes, in the Spirit, through that door he sees a throne in heaven. On the throne Someone is sitting, but John does very little to describe that Someone. We can easily understand why, of course; God is indescribably glorious, and no picture, no description, could do him justice. That is certainly one reason why the second commandment forbids making images of God, and why we are not given any description here that would allow us to try to draw a picture of God. So, John sees, and tells us about, representations of glory. He can see just enough to know that the throne is occupied, but the glory blinds his eyes. In a nutshell, that is the point of these two chapters, especially chapter 4: to assure us that there is a God on the throne of heaven and that he is indescribably glorious. The universe is not the result of chance. It was not made by chance and it is not governed by chance. The persecutions, trials and tribulations that happen to the churches in chapters 2 and 3, and to all churches down the history of the world, are not the result of chance either. Nor are they just the result of some malevolent power, some sub-deity who has somehow wrestled the throne from the hands of God and now has that power himself. No; the one on the throne is undoubtedly the great and glorious God. Suffering churches in particular need to know that there is a God in heaven who is still on the throne; how else are they going to go 'plodding on' week after week, year after year? When just naming the name of Christ can be fatal they have to know that there is a King on the throne, and we need that same knowledge as we face all that the world and our mortality can throw at us. Are we mocked for being Christians? Are we suffering the pain of bereavement? Is long-term illness spoiling our lives? These things are not tragic accidents; they are not outside the control of God. There is a King on the throne.

But it is not just suffering churches (and suffering Christians) that need this reminder; working churches need it too. The great temptation for God's people at all times is to give up, to slow down, not to work as hard as we used to, to forget that our faith and our work matter. If we are going to remember that they do matter, we need to know that there is a throne. If we are to regain any confidence in the success of the work that we are doing, we need to know that God is on that throne. There is still a throne in heaven—hallelujah.

The glory and majesty of the one on the throne is described for us in picture language in verses 3–5. The one who sat there had the appearance of jasper and carnelian. 'Jasper' is meaningless to most of us, and is very probably a poor translation anyway. John is describing a clear, white diamond, a stone that declares the glory and majesty of God. The carnelian is a blood-red, precious stone, and its appearance here speaks of the judgement of God. God is always presented in the Bible as a God of enormous glory and righteous judgement. In verse 5 we see from the throne flashes of lightning and hear the rumblings and peals of thunder. This points us back to the book of Exodus. When the people drew close to Mount Sinai and the presence of God, there were flashes of lightning and rumbles of thunder and the people in terror cried out in fear. They asked Moses to act as intermediary so that God would not speak to them directly again (Exodus 20:18–19). It is the same God who is here, accompanied again by peals of thunder and flashes of lightning. The judgement and the glory of God are seen together.

Over the throne is an emerald rainbow. How can a multi-coloured rainbow be green? We have to understand, I think, that John, though under the inspiration of the Spirit, is struggling to describe what he sees. So he sees a glistening bow, multi-coloured, but multi-colours of green; it is an emerald rainbow. More important than the colour of the rainbow is the meaning of rainbows in Scripture. The very first rainbow appeared after the great flood (Genesis 9:13) and was the sign of God's promise never again to flood the world. Now there is a rainbow in heaven: God has kept that promise, a promise he made in grace. Though God is great and glorious and holy to judge, yet the presence of a rainbow promises us that he is still a God of great mercy, a God who always keeps his covenant.

Around the throne there are twenty four other thrones. On these thrones are twenty-four elders. They are dressed in white and they have crowns of gold on their head. There is something special about them; they are pure and they are kings. Who are they? The clue is in the number: twenty-four. In the Old Testament there were twelve tribes; in the New Testament there were twelve apostles. These twenty-four elders represent the people of God under both the Old Covenant and the New Covenant.

Beyond them and a little further from the throne are four creatures, and what amazing creatures they are. They are covered in eyes front and back, and the first one looks like a lion, and the second like an ox. The third looks like a man, the fourth a flying eagle. Perhaps they speak in turn of nobility, strength, intelligence and far-sightedness. We do know what these creatures are because the prophet Ezekiel tells us. He sees these same creatures and describes them in Ezekiel 1:5 and 10:20. He tells us that they are cherubim—high-ranking angelic beings. Here in Revelation, though they are round the throne as well, notice that they are further from the throne than the elders. Why is that? Because the redeemed people of God are exalted to a position higher than that of even the highest angels. 'Do you not know,' says Paul writing to the Corinthians (1 Corinthians 6:3), 'that we will judge angels?' We, as redeemed people, are over the angels; they are ministering spirits, sent to those who are the heirs of salvation (Hebrews 1.14). These strange but glorious beings then are around the throne of God, but not as close to it (or to him!) as redeemed humanity is.

What do they do, these strange beings? Like the seraphim in Isaiah 6, they have six wings, and like those seraphim too they cry 'Holy, holy, holy is the Lord God Almighty, who was and is and is to come.' Heaven resounds with the praise of God! What are the elders doing? Whenever the living creatures give glory honour and thanks to him who sits on the throne, the twenty-four elders fall down before him who sits on the throne, and they too worship him, and they lay their crowns before him and they say 'You are worthy, our Lord and God to receive glory and honour and power; for you created all things and by your will they were created and have their being. '

'You are worthy' they cry. What is it that makes God worthy? What is it that fills these elders with praise, and fills heaven itself with praise? It is the fact that God is sovereign Lord: 'because you created all things and by your will they were created and have their being.' That is to say, everything that exists was brought into being by God. Everything that exists was brought into being to do the will of God. The whole universe is explained in this: we are here to do God's will. We are here to bring God praise and glory, for he is worthy of praise. Creation was brought into being in order that he might receive the praise that is his due.

## The Lamb on the throne

At first sight, there seems to be nothing new here. We can almost imagine

John saying 'That's fine, Lord; but none of this is anything new. I don't quite know why I had to come through the door into heaven for all this. The cherubim are there in Ezekiel, and I've read Ezekiel. And this whole vision of heaven is very much like the vision of heaven that Isaiah had, and I know Isaiah chapter six quite well, too. Why have you brought me into heaven? This is very familiar stuff; can you not tell me something new?'

Then it is as if God says to him 'Oh, yes; I can. Come with me a little further. I will show you something Isaiah could not tell you. For on the throne is—the Lamb.'

We would expect God the Father to be on the throne, and we have seen him there. Chapter 4 is all about the Father; it is only the *voice* of Jesus we heard. The second person of the Holy Trinity has hardly been mentioned at all, apart from his voice. But here as we move into chapter five, things are seen more clearly. Let us follow what we are told. We see the right hand of him who sits on the throne, and that is still the right hand of the Father. In his right hand he has a scroll, and that scroll seems to represent future history. When it is unfolded in the following chapters, the future of the earth and particularly the future of the church of God is revealed. The scroll is God's plan, God's purpose. It is written down because God knows what is going to happen; more than that, God has *planned* the future.

But there appears to be a problem with God's plan. That scroll is sealed with seven seals. The seals need to be opened before God's purpose can unfold. So an angel cries out, 'Who is worthy to break the seals?' Are there any volunteers? Is there anyone with enough power and glory to open the scroll? And there is a dramatic silence in heaven and earth and under the earth. It seems as if there is no-one. No-one is worthy; no-one has the power, no-one has the authority, no-one has the glory even to look inside the scroll. So John weeps, because he knows that this is important. He knows that this is the whole purpose of God. He knows that if God's will is to be done in the world, somehow this scroll has to be unrolled. Yet there is no-one who can come and undo it. One of the strongest Greek words for weeping is used here: John wails , he howls, because there is no-one worthy of opening the scroll. Then one of the elders says to him in effect, 'Calm down. Calm down. There is no need to wail. See—the Lion of the Tribe of Judah has triumphed. He is able to open the scroll.'

In the original Greek, the elder's words read much stronger than they do in our translation. Literally, it reads 'TRIUMPHED has the Lion of the Tribe of Judah.' TRIUMPHED! All the emphasis is on that. There has been a battle. And one—the Lion of the tribe of Judah—has been victorious in the battle and shown that he is worthy and able and powerful enough to undo these seals and unroll this scroll. '*Triumphed* has the Lion of the tribe of Judah!' There is no object to the sentence; it does not tell us what he has triumphed over. What HAS he triumphed over? Everything! That is the effect of having no object in the sentence here. The Lion has won the greatest victory of them all. The ultimate triumph is his. To emphasise this even more, the verb is in the aorist tense. That is a tense we do not have in English; it speaks of an action in the past that is completed for ever. The triumph is over; it is finished. The battle is won and will never have to be fought again. Not only has the Lion triumphed, he has triumphed once and for all time. So John's fears are calmed, and he turns to see this triumphant Lion.

Then comes one of the most dramatic moments in the whole of literature. John turns expecting to see a Lion, but he does not see a Lion. He sees a Lamb. The Lion of Judah is never mentioned again in the Book of Revelation. But the Lamb is there, and the Lion and the Lamb are one and the same. Not only does John see a Lamb, though; he sees a Lamb looking as if he had been slain. In this dramatic way we are reminded—if we need to be reminded—how our Lord Jesus Christ triumphed. He triumphed by dying; and now he is in the centre of the throne.

William Hendriksen's commentary on Revelation takes this as meaning 'in the midst of the throne area' and so he puts the Lamb between the four living creatures and the twenty-four elders. But I think Hendriksen is wrong at this point. The text of the NIV says '…standing in the centre of the throne' and that, I am sure, is what it means: the Lamb is on the throne.

But it seems that he has only just arrived there; we can almost say he is still moving. Verse 7 tells us that the one who is in the centre of the throne came and took the scroll from the right hand of him who sat on the throne. Here then is the Father sitting on the throne with the Lamb of God, who has triumphed, approaching him. This imagery is taken from the prophet Daniel, which speaks of the King of Glory ('one like the Son of Man') approaching the Ancient of Days (Daniel 7:13). It is a description of the ascension, when Christ—having completed his work, having triumphed, having cried out on the cross 'It is finished! I have triumphed'—ascends to his Father, passing through the heavens to the highest place in heaven. He takes his seat on the throne and then reaches out to his Father, taking from his Father's right hand the scroll of his Father's plans.

This is a most dramatic moment! It is not too strong to say that heaven has been waiting an eternity for this moment. This is the moment when the Son of God, who has become the Son of Man, ascends as man, sits on the throne and takes the right to unseal humanity's destiny. Psalm twenty-four prophecies of this moment: 'Lift up your heads, O you gates … that the King of Glory may come in. Who is this King of Glory? The Lord strong and mighty, the Lord mighty in battle … the Lord Almighty, he is the King of Glory' (verse 7–10). Now all of heaven thrills because at last the moment has arrived.

For us here on earth, when we have been waiting and waiting for something to happen, it is often an anticlimax. Think of the child counting the days to Christmas Day, waking with joy to a host of new toys—but then losing interest before the day is out. But that anticlimax is because we live in a fallen world, and because nothing on earth can ever really satisfy us. But there is no anticlimax in heaven. This moment that all heaven has been waiting for throughout all eternity has at last arrived, and all heaven erupts with a new song.

Before we notice the song, let us stay a moment with the Lamb. He is a very strange lamb, a lamb with horns. Horns are symbols of power and authority. He has seven eyes, and eyes are symbols of knowledge. Therefore he is a Lamb who knows all things, and has all authority—just as he said: 'All authority in heaven and earth has been given to me. Therefore go and make disciples of all nations' (Matthew 28:18). He is the One who has authority.

This is an amazing thing. When human nations look for figures of authority, Russia chooses a bear as its symbol. England takes a Lion; the United States takes an Eagle. God however takes a Lamb, and a slain lamb, a bleeding lamb, at that. 'This,' he says, 'is where true authority lies.'

Pause a moment, and think. Can you begin to grasp how the Christians in Ephesus and Thyatira and all those other places would have felt? When they refused to bow their knee to the Lordship of Caesar they are fiercely persecuted, tormented and tortured even to the point of death. Now the voice of Jesus himself reminds them that they are right not to submit. True power—the horn of authority—belongs to the Lamb.

## The Song

So that moment, awaited for all eternity, has at last arrived and a new song begins. It has to be a new song because a new situation has come into being. It is a song that Isaiah's angels could not sing, though Isaiah certainly prophesied about this moment. The new song is this: 'you are worthy to take the scroll and to open its seals, because you were slain, and with your blood you purchased men for God from every tribe and language and people and nation. You have made them to be a kingdom and priests to serve our God, and they will reign on the earth.'

Let me just say in passing, the Authorised Version is misleading here. It has 'and has redeemed us to God by thy blood.' But if you look carefully, the four living creatures and the twenty-four elders are all singing this song, and the four living creatures cannot say 'You have redeemed us ... by thy blood ...' Those creatures were not redeemed. The New International Version is quite right when it says 'men for God from every tribe ...'

Heaven then erupts with praise to God. Notice that as the elders sang of the sovereign honour and power and glory of God at the end of chapter four, so here they all sing about the work of Christ as being an *effective* work. 'You were slain and with your blood you purchased men for God.' They do not sing, 'you made their purchase possible, you made their redemption possible.' When the Bible speaks of the death of Christ, its language is always stronger than that. The language of the Bible about redemption always says that Christ's work is an effective work. It never suggests that redemption depends on human beings adding their part. It never suggests that Christ has done all he can, and now we must bring our faith before his work can be effective. Many Christians, if they were picturing salvation in modern terms, might say something like this. 'Faith is like petrol, and without the petrol the engine cannot start. Or it is like electricity and without electricity the light-bulb won't glow.' Both of those pictures are acceptable as far as they go, but only if we realise that the faith—the petrol or electricity—is itself part of the gift of God in Christ. It is part of the salvation that Christ has won for us. It is not that Christ has done all this and now we have to bring *our* faith. Christ has purchased us, redeemed us, bought us. As part of his dowry—as it were—he gives to us repentance and faith. (If this is a new idea for you, check it out: see Acts 11:18 where we are told that repentance is something God gives, and Ephesians 2:8 where the same point is made about faith.) Repentance and faith are not our contribution that we bring to God to make his work effective, as if poor God would have his whole purpose frustrated unless we did our bit. What a tuneless song that would produce:, 'By your blood you have made redemption possible.' That would be awful! We could never set that to music and it would not be worth singing if we did. God has an elect people, and his Son purchased their salvation and his Spirit calls them effectually to salvation in Christ. 'You by your blood *purchased* them for God.' To whom do they belong to now? 'I have revealed you to those whom you gave me out of the world. They were yours; you gave them to me,' says our Lord Jesus in John 17:6. 'All that the Father gives me will come to me, and whoever comes to me I will never drive away' (John 6:37). Purchased; redeemed, ransomed. It is finished!

We might say that this small group of four living creatures and twenty-four elders are God's soloists. Then as the picture moves on the whole choir stands, a choir numbering many thousands. If you really want to know, says John, there are ten thousand times ten thousand singing: a choir of a hundred million. It seems that the choir master of heaven has no problems recruiting his singers!

We will see repeatedly that the numbers in Revelation are symbolic. What is the point of this figure? When we get to 9:16 we will see that the enemies of God number two hundred million. Presumably that number is symbolic too; and it is a vast number, but we need not be concerned. God's choir alone is half that size, says the Lord, before we even begin to count the warriors! The 'band up front' is one hundred million! Now this vast choir begins to sing as well, and they too begin to sing 'worthy is the Lamb that was slain.' So all of heaven bursts forth in song, praising the king of glory.

But that isn't all; there is more to come. We have had (as it were) the soloists, and then the choir. Now, in the same way that the conductor at the

'Last Night of the Proms' turns to the audience and begins to conduct them, so heaven's choir master turns now to all creation and they all begin to sing: 'Every creature in heaven and on earth and under the earth and on the sea and all that is in them…' They all sing the same song: 'To him who sits on the throne and to the Lamb be praise and honour and glory and power for ever and ever.' Every creature joins in, fulfilling the promise of God that every tongue will confess that Jesus Christ is Lord to the glory of God the Father (Philippians 2:11).

When that heavenly choir master turns to that congregation, every one of us will all be joining in that song. Whether we are in heaven at that time, or in hell, we will sing. Did you notice that even hell sings his glory? 'Every creature in heaven and on earth and *under the earth* …' Now I have no doubt that those in hell are not singing his glory willingly, or joyfully; it must be a reluctant song. But even the fiends in hell itself have to admit that our Lord Jesus Christ is worthy of praise and honour and glory and power for ever and ever.

How far this puts us from modern pluralism! We are told relentlessly that all Gods—or should that be gods?—are the same, that it does not matter who we worship or how we worship, or even whether we worship at all. 'You can worship your God your way, and I'll worship my God my way: it's all the same in the end.' No. The Bible says that all earth, all heaven, all the sea, all alike will sing praise to the same Lamb. There will be no voices praising Mohammed or Buddha or Krishna. All will sing to the Father and to the Son. And those who sing among the redeemed will be from every people. His work is not just an effective work, it is an effective work among every tribe and language and people and nation. That is why the New Tribes Mission has as a motto 'Reaching every tribe until the last tribe is reached.' The Lord Jesus Christ will not return until every tribe has been reached; the Father has promised that the redeemed will include people from every tribe who will sing to the glory of the Lamb.

Then all the living creatures cry 'Amen'—which means: let it be. It means 'Bring it to pass.' It means 'It's the truth'. All those ideas are contained in the familiar word 'Amen'. What a day we are promised here; what a song that will be.

Before that day comes, the earth will have suffered much. The saints will have endured much tribulation. But here we get a vision of what it will be like when all that suffering is over and finished for ever. This is the beginning of the end. The victory song has begun; the Lamb has triumphed. He has won the right to unfold his Father's purpose; now we will see that victory unfold.

# Apocalypse now?

Please read Revelation chapters 6 and 7

## Where is history going?

**Marx** says history is going up and down—making progress by revolution. The ruling classes are overthrown by the downtrodden; they in turn become a new ruling class that misuses the poor. Eventually the poor rise up and overthrow their new rulers—and the world goes on and on. Oppression and revolution, up and down—but the day is coming when at last the true common people will enjoy power; we are heading for it and we will get there. Then what?

**Many Eastern religions** say history goes round and round: time is circular, life is circular—we are born, we die, we are re-incarnated (perhaps higher, perhaps lower) but history is a circle. The best we can hope for is one day to be lost in the great sea of nothingness that is Nirvana, when everything that makes us individual ceases to be and we are just like a droplet lost in the ocean.

**Much modern thinking** is even less optimistic; it says 'Nowhere.' History is pointless and life is pointless; a tale told by an idiot, full of sound and fury, signifying nothing. Though they are Shakespeare's words and around four hundred years old, they summarise the depression that characterises many people today. Everything is pointless; and because we cannot live like that, we have to give point to our own existence somehow by achieving experience, by making our mark. It may be by drugs, sex, violence or even—if we are very peculiar—by a life of self-sacrifice. But in the end, whatever we do to make our mark and get our experience, it is all pointless. History is going nowhere, and it means nothing. Nothing means anything at all.

**The bible says:** history is heading straight like an arrow for The Day of the Lord. Time is linear; it had a beginning and it will have an end. There are no replays, there is no reincarnation. In between the beginning and the end, time progresses constantly and relentlessly towards that end which will, surely and inevitably, come.

It is that view of history that shapes Revelation, and in chapter 6 we are given a little picture of how history feels to us, as well as how it looks to God. Then, in chapter 7, an interlude gives us a glimpse of heaven before we get back, in 8:1, to the seven seals that are mentioned here in the first verse of chapter 6.

Again, let me say that to understand Revelation properly we must grasp that it shows us a succession of parallel visions; I will keep repeating this because it is so important. The same great period in history, from the birth of our Lord Jesus Christ to his return in glory, is viewed several times from different perspectives. Here in chapter 6 we have a vision showing seven seals. They are followed by a vision in which seven trumpets sound, beginning in chapter 8. Chapters 12–14 show us the persecution of the church by the dragon and the beasts; then chapter 15 introduces seven bowls with seven plagues, and so on. But all of these visions are parallel, not consecutive. That means that we cannot go from the vision of heaven at the end of chapter 7 to the plagues beginning in chapter 8 and think 'This is what happens next.' Rather, John turns around and sees another representation of the same period in history. Yet it is also true that with each succeeding section the pace gets faster and we edge a little closer to the End, as we shall see.

In our last chapter, we saw a throne in heaven, and the Lord Jesus Christ as the slain and victorious Lamb, seated in the midst of the throne. By his death and resurrection he has conquered sin and death once and for all, and has achieved the right to open the seals on the scroll—that is, to unfold the purpose of God.

As we see those seals opened in chapter 6, they portray events so horrific that it is very difficult to remember that it is the Lamb, the Prince of Peace, that opens those seals. Revelation 6 is about a series of crises; the first four seals deal with the famous four horsemen of the Apocalypse ('Apocalypse' in this context is just another name for the Book of Revelation). Let us look at these crises.

## The crises

The first seal is opened and John sees before him a white horse. The voice of one of the four living creatures before the throne says 'Come' and a rider on a white horse rides out of heaven. His rider holds a bow and is given a crown, and he rides out, we are told, 'as a conqueror bent on conquest.' Who is this rider? This is one of the places where there is a fundamental disagreement amongst the interpreters.

Many good commentators say that this rider on the white horse is the Lord Jesus Christ. Their reasoning is that in Revelation 19 there is also a white horse and its rider is undoubtedly the Lord Jesus Christ. That is the only other time a white horse is mentioned in Revelation, so why imagine that here it is a different one? Furthermore, white is traditionally a symbol of purity, and on every other occasion when the colour white is mentioned in Revelation it is a symbol of heavenly things. So why should that be different here?

But, says another group of equally able commentators, that cannot be right. Firstly, they say, John has just too high a view of Jesus to list him as merely 'one rider amongst four'. For John, Jesus is always in a category all on his own. He could not even be 'the chief among four'; he is always on his own. While Jesus certainly receives his authority from the Father (see Matthew 28:18), it would simply be misleading to present him as 'given' power in the same way that the other horsemen are (verses 2,4,8). And if the Lamb opens the seal; how can he then also ride out of the seal? Most telling of all, they point out, each of the horses seems to bring disaster with it.

Which is right? It is certainly possible to see this rider as the Lord Jesus himself. The vision then represents his gospel as conquering the world but being continually attacked and opposed as it spreads. We cannot deny that this would be a very true picture! But on balance I think the second interpretation is best; I suspect that this rider does not represent Jesus, but a false conqueror. It represents a spirit of imperialism, holding out a warning of nations building power and empires. That, too, is a true picture; it has been the history of the world since time immemorial. An Empire arises, it conquers large parts of the world and begins to see itself as invincible. But then its power fades, and the Empire is taken over by another. John is seeing this vision at the time of the Roman Empire, and a white horse is a fitting symbol of the Roman Empire, because their victorious generals would return to Rome on white horses. God wants us to see that throughout history there will always be nations that grow in power and build empires.

He wants us to be aware that those empires will generally bring disaster, and be opponents of the Christian faith even as the Roman Empire was. But those empires will never last; it is only the kingdom of Jesus that lasts for ever. John's readers are given a hint that the Roman Empire itself—so powerfully oppressing Christians when the vision is given—is not going to last very much longer. The rider of this horse carries a bow, and the bow was not a Roman weapon. That is the hint; imperialism will always exist, but the Roman Empire will soon fall and be followed by another empire waging war with different weapons.

This past century is very familiar with imperialism. The British Empire of the 19th century claimed to be the 'Empire on which the Sun never sets'. The white horse in the 20th century would include Nazism, which set out to build an empire that would last a thousand years: but it did not last more than a dozen. Then communism arose, and saw itself as the great End to which all history had been aiming. Now, that too has crumbled. Yet still there are others on a continual rush to capture territory, with all the pain and tragedy that brings. Yes, says God to John, there will always be empires; there will always be a new white horse.

Then the Lamb opens the second seal. The second living creature calls a horse out from that seal, and this horse is fiery red. That is appropriate; red is the colour of war, and this rider has the power to take peace from the earth. This horse seems to represent anarchy and civil war.

To get a clue as to what is happening here, we examine the words at the end of the verse. 'To him was given a large sword.' Now, that is a strange translation, for the word used for sword here is machaira, which Vine[1] defines as 'a short sword or dagger.' Then, John gives it an adjective, 'megas'—which means big. So we are told that this rider carries a 'big little sword.' So what is John telling us? I think it means a large dagger; an assassin's dagger, perhaps; a dagger that an assassin can easily carry in his robes. But it is certainly 'mega' in its impact on the world if it is used to slay an emperor. That seems to fit well with what we are told; this rider takes peace from the earth. When Empires spread, they spread by war; but ironically they often bring a kind of peace with them. People used to talk about the Pax Romana—the Roman Peace. The Roman Empire brought Roman Law. It was an empire that seemed to be invincible, and nations did not rise against it and its law unless they were suicidal. Roman Peace. But when empires begin to crumble, even an oppressive empire, wars can multiply. John's readers would remember that following Nero's reign—and Nero was a fanatic, a mad man of the worst kind—there were four emperors in one year, and a perpetual threat throughout the Empire of civil war. We may have noticed ourselves in our own day that the collapse of the Soviet Union has broken the fragile peace that existed, and wars have multiplied. We speak about the end of the Cold War, but we have moved into a series of very active wars.

The third seal brings out a third horsemen. 'I heard the third living creature say "Come!" ... and there before me was a black horse.' This seems to represent famine—or at least, rampant inflation. Its rider is holding a pair of scales in its hand, and there is a voice from the four living creatures saying 'A quart of wheat for a day's wages, and three quarts of barley for a day's wages, and do not damage the oil and the wine.' A quart of wheat was a day's ration; what is represented here is economic hardship. A man has to work all day and can just about afford to eat for the day with what he has earned. Barley is not of the same quality; he can subsist for a day on quart of barley, so if he has a family he will have to buy three quarts of barley for a day's wages; then (provided he only has a wife and one child) they are just about all right! Life itself—mere existence—has become a struggle.

What about 'Do not damage the oil and the wine'? How you interpret that may depend in part on your own political views! It could be a reference to the way the rich continue to enjoy their pleasures when the poor can barely eat; we see that so many times. The rich have their luxuries still, while there are other people dying in the streets, just beyond their gates. 'I know there are poor people out there, old chap. But don't let it spoil our banquet!' If your politics are different, though, you may see it referring to something else we often see: when the poor, while lamenting their lack of material resources, still will not give up their luxuries (in our day, perhaps, smoking and drinking and colour televisions) even when the family is on the poverty line.

Perhaps we can admit, for the purposes of this chapter, that there is some truth in both of those views? Either way, the sinfulness of humanity is showed to us. The reality of economic injustice is fuelled by ongoing sin.

Then there is a fourth seal. 'The fourth living creature says 'Come!' ... and there before me was a pale horse.' While most of the translations say 'pale horse' the word is 'chloros'—from which we get the words chlorine and chlorophyll. It means green; it is sickly green—the green of impending death. 'My, you're looking green around the gills,' we might say to someone. We do not mean that they are looking healthy! That is the kind of green mentioned here; it represents famine and plague spreading throughout the world, even to a fourth of the earth. Death and Hades follow close behind this horse; death and the grave swallow up wherever he goes. Power is given to kill a fourth of the earth—by sword, famine, plague and the wild beasts of the earth.

Plague has always been a reality. In the fourteenth century 25 million people were killed by Black Death in Europe. In those days, Europe was not as populous as it is now; 25 million was a very significant proportion. In the nineteenth century, ten million died in the Far East of Bubonic Plague in one decade, the 1890s. We still talk about epidemics; we very rarely (thank God!) see pandemics. But we cannot be sure they have gone for ever; as I write this, a television news item has just reported the view of some scientists that the Black Death itself is only lying dormant, ready to wreak havoc again in the future.

What about the wild beasts? Some ecologists are seriously suggesting that the balance of nature in some parts of the world has turned already. Because of economic injustice and poverty, and because of the greed of the rich who continue polluting the atmosphere and destroying the rain forests, then, they tell us, ecological disaster is staring us in the face. Man is ill-equipped to survive and will (some doom merchants tell us) be destroyed by the wild beasts.

Whether you think that is likely or not, it is interesting that each of these four apocalyptic pictures seems more credible now than ever they have before. Having seen so many technological advances that give us much cause for thanksgiving, but also bring many serious problems, we can believe far more easily than our great-grandfathers could in global disasters. Even non-Christians take the four horsemen of the apocalypse seriously and produce books and studies with that title, speaking about the doom of the earth.

Is all this a sign that the end is upon us? Not necessarily; these are not signs of the end! This is what life is going to be like throughout all of history.

To confirm this, you might like to read Matthew 24, and note the close parallels between these seals and what we are told there. It is a common misunderstanding that 'wars and rumours of wars' are signs that the end is near. But Jesus teaches the exact opposite (verse 6: 'the end is still to come'). These he says are the birth pangs; signs of the beginning, not the end. When Christ ascended into glory, then the seals began to be opened, and we have been seeing those seals opened down the centuries ever since.

John says (1 John 2:18): 'Dear children, this is the last hour; and as you have heard that the antichrist is coming, even now many antichrists have come. This is how we know it is the last hour.' John believed he was writing in the last hour, and he was. How does he know it is the last hour? Because anti-Christian activity was going on around him all the time. That is a characteristic of the whole period between the first and second comings of our Lord Jesus Christ. Hunger, sickness, death and injustice will continue to the end.

That does not mean that Christians can be complacent. It certainly does not mean that we should sit on our hands and say 'If they are going to happen to the very end it would be sinful to try and do anything about them.' This is not the way Christians reason! In fact the reverse is true; Christians have always been at the forefront of movements to alleviate suffering. As an example, you might like to consult 'AD'—a booklet produced by Day One and the FIEC to mark the new millennium.[2] In it, the authors trace numerous influential Christians who have made a difference to justice and suffering in the world. Just to take one example from our own day, ACET (Aids Care Education and Training) was founded in 1988 as a Christian response to HIV and AIDS. As well as becoming one of the leading independent providers of sexual health education in secondary schools, it is estimated that ACET has cared for almost one in ten of the people in the UK ill or dying with AIDS. Similar examples could be multiplied; complacency and resignation to 'the will of God' is never the proper Christian response to other people's suffering. Yet whatever we may do, things will not get significantly better for the world or the church. Hunger, sickness, death and injustice will continue.

Inevitably we respond to this by crying out 'O Lord, how long?' That is exactly what happens when the fifth seal is opened. John sees under the altar the souls of those who had been slain because of the word of God and the testimony they had maintained. They called out in a loud voice, 'How Long, Sovereign Lord, holy and true, until you judge the inhabitants of the earth and avenge our blood?'

Many Christians believe that those in heaven cannot see what is going on on the earth, but this passage seems to indicate that they are wrong. It seems very clear that those under the altar know that great disasters are happening on the earth. They know particularly that Christian people, their brothers and sisters, are still suffering, and it is in response to that they cry out 'How long?' What answer are they given? 'They were told to wait a little while longer, until the number of their fellow-servants and brothers who were to be killed as they had been was completed.' It is still not time for them to know the times and seasons!

Beware of those who say they have worked out—even approximately— the date of the End. We know there have been many attempts in the past and still today. For example, many of us remember the days before electronic calculators when we had to use logarithms to work out our long multiplications and divisions. Logarithms were invented by a man named Napier, and Napier wrote a very popular commentary on Revelation, proving that Christ would return between 1688 and 1700. It was a very popular book, and sold extremely well—until 1701! All such attempts to date the Second Coming have been proved wrong. That is partly because the disasters spoken of in these seals are not the end. We are not being helped to work out the date of our Lord's return, but warned about the world's state and fate.

Then the sixth seal is opened. There is a great earthquake and the sun turns black, like sackcloth made of goat hair. All this imagery speaks of cosmic upheaval. It may only be a literary device, telling us that something so radical is going to happen that the world has never seen its like before. But I think not; while it cannot be literal (moon *literally* turning to blood; stars *literally* falling to the earth), this is the imagery that the Bible reserves for the end of the world. Joel 2:30–31 prophecies this;[3] Peter's words that 'the elements will melt in the heat' (2 Peter 3.12) seem to echo this. The world as we know it will come to an end. And when it does—when the sky recedes like a scroll rolling up and the mountains and islands are removed from their place—then it will not matter whether you are rich or poor, slave or freeman, king, prince or general. All those hid in the caves among the mountains and called the mountains and rocks to fall on them and hide them from the wrath of ... the Lamb.

Pause for a moment, and think about that phrase and the picture it conjures up. An angry lamb. It would be ludicrous; but this is no ordinary lamb. This is the Lion of the Tribe of Judah. We need to remember that earthly greatness and earthly kingdoms count for little. In fact, in that day they will count for nothing. Samuel Rutherford, a great Scottish Presbyterian preacher of the seventeenth century, managed to offend the English King many times by his faithfulness to the gospel. While he was on his deathbed in 1661, Rutherford received a summons to appear before the king on a particular date. Rutherford sent the servant back, saying 'I must answer my first summons; and before your day arrives, I will be where few kings and great folks come.' In the end, there is only one King that matters. When this great day of wrath is revealed, who can stand?

Many people object violently to the idea of God's wrath today and Christians often find themselves on the defensive. We need to remember that usually when people take objection to the idea of God being angry, usually what they mean is 'Why won't God leave me alone to enjoy my sin?' But a holy God could never do that; it is just not possible to be truly good without being angry at evil.

Then, suddenly we are in chapter seven. We have not reached the seventh seal; there is a delay in heaven we are told (8:1); and in chapter 7 we see into heaven and we see the redeemed of the Lord. In fact, we see two redeemed multitudes. The question has been asked, 'Who can stand now that the great day of wrath has come?' (see 6:17) and so we need an assurance that some will be able to stand. That assurance is what we get in chapter 7.

All the warnings we have read tell us that life itself is not going to be easy, and the coming judgement is going to be harder still. But before those final judgements fall, before the seventh seal is opened and the wrath of the Lamb is made known, the angels have to hold back the six winds of the earth until another angel has come from the east 'having the seal of the

Living God.' He gives a command to the four angels who have been given power to harm the land and the sea, 'Do not start judgement until we have put a seal on the foreheads of the servants of God.' The seal represents security and ownership. Here, it has the same function as the Passover blood in Exodus 12. In that chapter, the Angel of Death passed through the land and wherever he saw the blood on a doorpost, he would pass over that house. All inside were allowed to live; they belonged to God and the blood was his seal. Now, there is a seal on the heads of all God's people, so that the great judgements to come cannot hurt them.

All of God's people are sealed by the Spirit. In the Scripture, the seal is not an experience that comes after conversion. There are (of course!) experiences of God that come after conversion. But the seal of the Spirit is the mark of God's ownership: '[God] set his seal of ownership on us, and put his Spirit in our hearts as a deposit, guaranteeing what is to come' (2 Corinthians 1:22). If the Spirit is in your heart, you have God's seal of ownership on you. If the Spirit is not in your heart, you do not yet belong to Christ (Romans 8:9). 'Having believed, you were marked in him with a seal, the promised Holy Spirit who is a deposit guaranteeing our inheritance until the redemption of those who are God's possession—to the praise of his glory' (Ephesians 1:13–14). What is the seal? It is the Holy Spirit himself, who dwells in the hearts of believers.

So the angel goes through, putting the seal on the forehead. It is clearly visible. The Lord knows his own people, and none of them will be damaged; these judgements will not be allowed to hurt them.

But God's definition of what 'hurts' is not the same as ours! God's people may suffer in these judgements. They may even die in them, even by martyrdom, as empires rise and turn against Christ, as assassins destroy emperors and factions rise against Christian people. But all these things work together for the good of those who love God (Romans 8:28). Here we have a picture of that, with the redeemed in heaven. There are 144,000 of them, and behind them a great multitude that no-one could count.

That 144,000 is a symbolic number. It represents what Paul calls the Israel of God, the church of the OT and NT (Galatians 6:16). At first sight, it seems that the 144,000 represent Jewish believers, and the multitude behind represents Gentile believers in Christ. But if we want to be consistent in the book of Revelation, we cannot make that interpretation. In 14:1 and 14:3, it is clear that the 144,000 represents the whole multitude of redeemed from the earth. So the multitude seems to be the vision's way of saying 'Don't take the numbers too literally; they are only symbols. In reality, there is a great multitude that no man can number.' What we are seeing here is the fulfilment of God's promise to Abraham. In Genesis 15:5, God says to Abraham 'Look up and count the stars, if you can count them. So shall your offspring be!' God's promise is fulfilled. This is Abraham's unnumbered offspring. And all these people sing the praise of God, joining with the living creatures.

One of the elders says to John, 'Now John, where did all these in white robes come from?' They are holding palm branches in their hands; this is the heavenly Feast of Tabernacles. The Feast of Tabernacles is a time of celebration for the harvest; this is the last great harvest. This is the final victory of God; but where have these people come from? Reminiscent of Ezekiel 37, John seems unprepared to commit himself. When Ezekiel was asked 'Son of man, can these bones live?' he replied 'Sovereign Lord, you alone know.' Here John answers, 'Sir, you know.' 'You tell me,' says John. And the elder does: 'These are they who have come out of the great tribulation; they have washed their robes and made them white in the blood of the Lamb.'

## What is the great tribulation?
What is the great tribulation? It is quite simply earth as represented under these four horsemen. Some interpreters—particularly dispensationalists—see it as a particular time of terrible trouble close to the end. That is because they see Revelation 4–22 as consecutive, not parallel: so in their interpretations, the great tribulation has to be a particular period just before the opening of the seventh seal. But there are I think several things against that interpretation. The first is that, as I hope will become increasingly clear as we work through Revelation, these visions are parallel. Second, the Greek tense, called by one commentator[4] 'a timeless present' makes our translation not particularly helpful. Not 'these are they who *have come* ...' but 'these are they who *come* out of the great tribulation'—it is an ongoing thing. Thirdly, the Greek word translated

tribulation is 'thlipsis'—it is the same word used in John 16:33 which the Authorised Version translates: 'In this world you will have tribulation.' It simply describes the Christian life, a life of trouble. So the great tribulation is 'the awesome totality of tribulation which from century to century has been the experience of the people of God' (Hughes). Remember how the apostle describes the life of faith: 'Others were tortured and refused to be released, so that they might gain a better resurrection. Some faced jeers and flogging, while still others were chained and put in prison. They were stoned; they were sawn in two; they were put to death by the sword. They went about in sheepskins and goatskins, destitute, persecuted and ill-treated—the world was not worthy of them. They wandered in deserts and mountains, and in caves and holes in the ground' (Hebrews 11: 35–38).

The people in white robes, then, with palm branches before the throne. Where have they come from? They have come from a life of trouble on the earth. But on the earth, in the midst of that trouble, they have been faithful to God.

Are they sinless then? They are now, now that they are before the throne. But they were not sinless on earth; they did, however, wash their robes and make them white in the blood of the Lamb. They have been washed clean; they have been saved. This great multitude, this 144,000 and the number that no-one can count, these are those who are saved. Thank God, there is a lot of them! They have washed their robes; they are white robes, they are clean. Their sin is washed away. It is a strange picture: washing in blood, and coming out clean! But that is what happens when it is sin we are talking about, and the blood is the shed blood of Jesus. Those who come to him and put their faith in him, are washed in the blood.

We may well have reached days when in our witnessing, in our open air preaching and the like, it is no longer wise to talk about 'the blood of the Lamb.' I am not being unfaithful to Scripture; the apostles did not speak like that when preaching to Gentiles either. They knew it would be a meaningless phrase to those with no understanding of the Scriptures. So, it may be inappropriate in our witnessing to start here; but we can never forget. This is the only way we get into heaven!

It is a question we all need to ask ourselves, whatever we may have assumed. Have we washed *our* robes in the blood of the Lamb? Like Judas, we can have so many privileges and yet not be saved. There is a great multitude in heaven, and everyone of them has got there the same way: through Jesus, and his blood. No amount of understanding of the Book of Revelation would make up for this lack! No-one washes their robes in the Law of Moses; no-one washes them in the rites of Buddha; no-one washes them in the five pillars of Islam. All those in heaven are there because of the blood of Jesus. Are you forgiven? It is the only way to get there!

Now that they are there, they are before the throne of God in heaven and they serve him day and night. That just means for ever and ever; without a break. Later in Revelation (21:25) we are told that there is no night. But how else could we say it? They serve him in the temple, although there is no temple either (21:22)! It means: in his immediate presence; his tent is spread over them (15)—God himself is protecting them from all ills. They will never be hungry again and they will never be thirsty again. The Sun will never scorch them again—Psalm 121 speaks in just those terms. In heaven, that promise is fulfilled, for it is filled full.

And if the idea of the wrath of the Lamb was strange, here is another strange idea: the Lamb at the centre of the throne is the Shepherd (17). He leads them to springs of living water—as he always has: 'The Lord [Jehovah] is my shepherd; he leads me beside the still waters …' God is our shepherd; the Lamb is that great Jehovah. And throughout all eternity, he meets the needs of our souls. He leads us to the springs of living waters and God wipes away every tear from our eyes. Long before the feminists came on the scene, the Biblical writers knew that God is the great Mother, as well as the great Father. We do not call him Mother; we have no Biblical warrant for doing that. But still, he does the work of a Mother as he wipes away every tear we have ever wept.

These are the things that must soon come to pass. We live in the time of these seals. Do not let the world and its troubles get you down; there is a throne. There is a Lamb on the throne, and all that happens around us is part of the purpose of God. And you, if you are God's; if you are sealed; if you have his Spirit within you: you are protected always by that Spirit, by that blood, by that Father who loved you and gave his Son to be your Saviour. John's readers needed to hear that, and so do we.

**Notes**

1 **W.E. Vine,** *Expository Dictionary of New Testament Words* (Peabody: Hendrickson Publishing, no date)
2 **Brian Edwards and Ian Shaw,** *'AD'* (Epsom: Day One Publications, 1999).
3 The attentive reader will notice that Peter in Acts 2:17–21 quotes this passage and refers it to what is happening on the day of Pentecost. That is right: the last days begin with the ascension of the Lord Jesus and the outpouring of his Spirit; they end with 'the sun turned to darkness' and throughout that whole period, 'everyone who calls on the name of the Lord will be saved.'
4 **P.E. Hughes,** *The Book of the Revelation* (Leicester: IVP, 1990).

# How God answers the cries of his people

Please read Revelation Chapters 8 and 9

Every Christian would want to say that prayer is a precious gift. At the same time, we all know that there are many mysteries to do with prayer, and one of the greatest of them is that our prayers are not always answered. Sometimes, we pray and pray and pray and seem to get nowhere—even though we are as sure as we can be that we are asking for good things. We could understand it if we were praying to win the lottery! But however hard we try to pray for spiritual things, and to pray according to God's will, yet sometimes our prayers seem unanswered. Sometimes, indeed, things seem to get even worse when we pray!

When Christians are persecuted, they inevitably and rightly pray for God to intervene and protect them in their persecutions. Surely, we may think, if God is going to answer any prayers, then these will be the prayers he answers. Yet even then, sometimes it seems as if nothing happens. Great men of the gospel are imprisoned or killed, with multitudes of ordinary Christians and their families being cruelly persecuted.

This vision of the trumpets, in four chapters (8–11) deals with one such case of apparently unanswered prayers. God's people are being persecuted, and though there is much prayer, the persecution continues. Now we must remember that this is a vision and it is full of symbols. Once again many of the details are difficult, and we have to remind ourselves that Revelation is not next year's newspaper or a history book written in advance. That will not mean that we evacuate the symbols of their meaning, but it will mean that we try to get at their heart. And once again, in this chapter as in all the others, we are trying to get at the main picture, and we are not too concerned about every little detail.

So far, we have seen the vision of the seven seals and have seen the Lamb (the Lord Jesus Christ) open the seals. However, just as the last seal is opened, when we think judgement is about to begin and we are expecting the Lord Jesus Christ to burst through the heavens we switch, instead, to another series of visions. This time we see visions of seven trumpets. It is another look at history, but from a slightly different perspective; as we have seen, John's visions are to be taken as 'in parallel' rather than consecutive.

The question implied in this vision of trumpets is this: what does God do when his people cry out for deliverance? I suspect that some people reading this chapter may well be shocked by what they read; the Scripture reading itself is difficult! If you are shocked, I hope it is not because I am trying to shock you, but because the truths told in these chapters are themselves shocking—at least to minds that have not been well conditioned by the Scriptures. Sadly few of us, these days, have such minds. So let us remind ourselves before we plunge in that the whole Bible insists that God is a good, wise and gracious God who loves the world and always does what is right. Then we will be ready to see four things in this vision.

## 1. God does answer prayer

Although the suffering people of God may feel that their prayers are unanswered and maybe even unheard, God does answer the desperate cries of his people for deliverance. That seems to be the focus of these chapters.

Even if you have not been a Christian very long, you will know that there are many promises in the Bible about God answering prayer. 'Your Father knows what you need before you ask him' (Matthew 6:8). 'You may ask me for anything in my name, and I will do it' (John 14:14). 'This is the confidence we have in approaching God: that if we ask anything according to his will, he hears us' (1 John 5:14). Such promises could easily be multiplied over many pages, there are so many. And if we have been Christians for any length of time, we will have our stories to tell, stories of times when God answered prayers remarkably. (That is why I think testimonies—not just the story of our conversion, but other stories about God's dealings with us as his people, are very precious. We need to take more seriously the apostle's command to 'encourage one another with these words' [1 Thessalonians 4:18]).

We all have our stories. I remember shortly after my wife and I married, we were coming home from church one Sunday evening and driving her grandmother home, as we usually did. She was telling us about a time in her own early married life when she and her husband were so poor they literally sometimes did not know where their next meal was coming from. On this occasion they had a bill to pay and had no idea how they were going to pay it. They prayed, and told no-one but God. As they were praying the letter-box rattled, and when they went to see what had caused it there was an envelope waiting for them. In it—you will have guessed—was an amount of money that precisely met their need. It is by no means a unique story; if we were to ask all the readers of this chapter for their own experience, we would find such stories to be very common. Common, common but unspeakably precious. (Perhaps today with credit cards and bank loans and a culture that encourages debt, they are not perhaps as common as they used to be. It is one of the disadvantages of living in an affluent society.) When people tell us that faith is nonsense, and answers to prayer are just coincidences worked on by our imagination, we have to smile at their naiveté and ignorance. We know that God is real, and that he answers prayer.

So, with that in mind, back to the text. Chapter eight verse three tells us something about the prayers of the saints: 'Another angel, who had a golden censer, came and stood at the altar. He was given much incense to offer, with the prayers of all the saints, on the golden altar before the throne.' The incense these prayers are mingled with may well represent the prayers of our Lord Jesus Christ on our behalf who, according to Hebrews 7:25, 'always lives to intercede' for us. We are also told elsewhere (Romans 8:26) that the Spirit aids in our prayers because there are times when we do not know what to pray for. We are such weak creatures that we cannot even pray to God without the help of God; so our prayers are aided by the Spirit and assisted by the prayers of our Lord Jesus, just as these prayers are mingled with incense. Helped in this way, they rise into the presence of God. Then the angel takes the censer (holding the mingled prayer and incense) and he fills it with fire from the altar, which he then hurls onto the earth. Great judgements follow. They are heralded by peals of thunder and rumbling and flashes of lightning and an earthquake. Then seven angels with seven trumpets prepare to sound them. Perhaps you remember the children's chorus with the refrain 'The prayers go up and the blessings come down'? But here, the prayers go up and it is judgements that come down: God answers his people's prayer by inflicting judgements on those who oppress them. Pause and think about that for a moment, as it brings us to the second point that we must note.

## 2. God's judgements fall

In 8:1 there is a silence in heaven for about half-an-hour. That is our indication to reflect, as we move on from the seals to the trumpets. The trumpets do not follow the seals; it is another vision, parallel with the vision of the seven seals. Though we might have expected after chapter seven to proceed straight to the last judgement, we do not. There is silence, and then another vision begins.

The judgements spoken of in this vision of trumpets are severe, but they are still not 'the final judgement'. The final judgement will bring all things to an end, but this chapter tells us about judgements that destroy only (only!) a third of the earth; the word 'third' comes six times in verses 7–12.

The seven trumpets represent seven judgements. Because a trumpet call is a warning (Amos 3:6), these seven trumpets speak of warnings that God uses to call the world away from its sin, as we shall see.

The seven trumpets may be conveniently divided into two groups. The first group of four are linked together and describe environmental disasters, and the last three describe disasters that fall more directly on humanity. Then, very solemnly, in 9:20–21 we see the failure of those warnings.

So, open your Bibles and begin to follow me as we work our way through these trumpets, concentrating as always on the main points and paying little attention to the details.

## Four trumpets

Trumpet one speaks of the judgements falling on the land: hail and fire mixed with blood are hurled down on the earth. It is so severe that a third of the earth is burned, a third of the trees are burned and all the green grass is burned. Trumpet two heralds a huge mountain all ablaze being thrown into the sea so that a third of the sea turns into blood and a third of the living creatures die and a third of the ships are destroyed. The third trumpet heralds a great star falling from the sky like a blazing torch. The name of the star is 'Wormwood' which means bitterness, and a third of the waters—rivers and springs—turns bitter. This is a reference back to Jeremiah 9:15 which reads in the Authorised Version 'Behold, I will feed them, even this people, with wormwood, and give them water of gall to drink.' It is helpful of the NIV to translate this for us as 'bitter food'; but it does obscure the Revelation connection! Jeremiah explains (9:13) that God feeds with wormwood—with bitter waters and poisoned waters—the people who have turned away from his law. All of these judgements fall on those who have turned away from God and his ways.

In the last half century this has often been linked with nuclear fallout; and some tell us that 'Chernobyl' means 'wormwood'. Until April 1986, that would have meant nothing; Chernobyl was merely an obscure city in north-central Ukraine. But then on 26th April 1986 the number four reactor at the Lenin Nuclear Power Plant, twenty-five kilometres from Chernobyl yet called by its name, exploded. It released into the atmosphere thirty to forty times the combined radioactivity of the bombs dropped forty years earlier on Hiroshima and Nagasaki. Thirty-one people died immediately, but no-one knows what the final number of victims will be. Hundreds of thousands of people had to abandon entire cities within the worst-contaminated zone of thirty kilometres radius. Spotting that the meaning of 'Chernobyl' is 'Wormwood', inevitably some Christians were quick to point to that tragedy as *the* fulfilment of this text. Certainly, it seems rather close to be a 'mere' coincidence; but to say exclusively that 'this is that' seems to ignore the fact that Revelation is a book of symbols. Certainly it is a stark warning of the reality of environmental catastrophe, and nuclear fallout may be one manifestation of the judgement of God.

Then comes trumpet four: destruction in the heavens. These details are the hardest of all to interpret, but they complete the picture of the universe: the earth, the sea, the rivers and now the heavenly bodies themselves are affected by the judgement of God. There is nowhere—literally nowhere—where God's enemies can escape his judgement!

In a previous chapter we saw, as the seals were opened, persecution on the church again and again. We also saw (and heard) the saints from the altar crying out 'How long O Lord?' The saints of God cried out for deliverance, and now judgement falls and all creation is mobilised by God against those who persecute the church of God. That is the point: the suffering, persecuted church is seeing its prayers answered by judgement on the world. This then is the shocking thing: however dreadful these disasters (and the other three, called 'woes') are, they fall in answer to the prayers of the saints.

If you have ever studied the philosophy of religion you will know that a major topic is the so-called problem of evil: if there is a God who is both almighty and loving, how can you explain suffering in the world? Literally thousands of articles and books have been written about this, some by Christians, some by theists (who believe in God but are not genuine Christians), some by agnostics and some by atheists. But in all my reading on the subject, I have not seen one who even approaches this answer: that some of the sufferings of the world are not evidence *against* the existence of God but evidence *for* it, because he is judging those who persecute his church.

## Three woes

The final three trumpets herald three judgements that are so serious they are each described as 'woes'. Three times an eagle cries 'Woe', as if announcing each one of them in advance.

As we move into chapter nine, the first woe begins as the fifth trumpet sounds: another star falls to the abyss from heaven. This star is not the same as the first; this one is undoubtedly Satan, the devil, because we are told that his name is Abaddon or Apollyon, (9:11) which means 'destroyer', and that he is given the key to the shaft, the bottomless abyss. Remember our Lord Jesus Christ says (and we will see further reference to this later) 'I saw Satan fall like lightning from heaven' (Luke 10:18). Now, then, we are being introduced to Satan's activity in the world.

With Satan come great locusts, fearsome beasts, that represent his demons. They are locusts because they devour, and the effect of these locusts is terrible. Let us notice the gruesome picture: 'The locusts looked like horses prepared for battle. On their heads they wore something like crowns of gold, and their faces resembled human faces. Their hair was like women's hair, and their teeth were like lions' teeth. They had breastplates like breastplates of iron, and the sound of their wings was like the thundering of many horses and chariots rushing into battle. They had tails and stings like scorpions, and in their tails they had power to torment people for five months' (9:7–10). Can you visualise these creatures? They are enough to give anyone nightmares. But it is not their appearance that is most terrifying: it is their awesome power to cause havoc. During these days (verse 6) men will seek death but will not find it. They will long to die, but death will elude them. They are dreadful days, but (in God's goodness) there is a limit to them, and the limit is five months.

Some commentators work hard to explain the symbolism there. Five, they say, is half of ten. (So far, we are all in complete agreement!) In the Bible, ten is the number that symbolises completion or perfection, and so five is used to indicate that this destruction is not complete and does not go on for ever. It is just another way of saying 'for a limited period'. Not only is the period limited, but the victims of these fearsome creatures are limited as well. It is to those victims—or rather those who are not the victims—that we must turn in a moment.

William Hendriksen comments about a locust storm 'The destruction, the utter ruin, the desolation and despondency caused by a locust storm can only be understood by the person who has seen and experienced it. Under the symbolism of a locust plague, John describes the powers and influences of hell operating in the hearts and lives of wicked men.'[1] That is what we are introduced to. As we have seen, the leader of these hellish hordes is Abaddon, Apollyon, the Destroyer, Satan. Such is his power that those who feel it cry out for death. Notice that and notice it well: Satan persecutes his followers! He hates them; he does not love them. We are too easily deluded by 'the pleasures of sin.' Certainly sin is pleasurable—for a season. But the devil does not tempt us to sin because of the pleasure it may bring us. He is not an alternative Christ, seeking the well-being of those who follow him but with a different idea of what well-being is. He is instead a ferocious leader of a fearsome brood, who torments and persecutes—for as long as he is given power—all those who follow him. When men turn from God, they turn from one who would be their friend to one who would destroy them. That is the tragedy of humanity without Christ.

How does Satan damage them? The locust has stings like scorpions, we are told twice in the passage. Scorpions in Ezekiel 2 represent those who reject the word of God: false prophets who have their own supposed revelations. A world that rejects God's truth is driven to destruction and despair by poisonous heresies, falsehoods and infidelity—unfaithfulness, that is, to God. When Satan is let loose there is hopeless despair: look again at chapter nine verse six. 'During those days men will seek death but will not find it.' They will long to die but death will elude them; they are a people crying out for death. A worldview—a philosophy of life—that does not have God at the centre does not have hope; it leads to despair, destruction, and the hope of death!

It is said that the greatest cause of death among young people in both the US and the UK—and young men in particular—is suicide! Is that not appalling? We live in a society which is under the influence of Satan. It has shrugged off the golden chains of God's law expecting freedom, but found itself under poisonous and destructive heresies that lead only to despair and a crying out for death. Many, many despairing people take what seems to be the easy way out. Governments, it seems, are powerless to prevent it. They recognise the problem, but they cannot diagnose either its cause or its remedy. This is no great surprise! The governments themselves are dominated by the very same materialistic humanism that produces the despair that leads to suicide. They do not know what to begin to do.

That is the first woe; there are two others yet to come. Can anything be worse? Yes; there are two more woes to come, and the second woe is certainly worse than the first. It releases widespread death on mankind. A vast army of evil, two hundred million troops, is unleashed. Again, the details are very hard. But the main meaning is clear. Throughout the church age—throughout that whole period from the ascension of our Lord Jesus Christ to his return in glory—the Lord will answer the prayers of his people in such a way that their opponents—the opponents of the church of Christ—will suffer his judgement for the ways they have abused his chosen people. But the church itself is protected. Whatever is happening here, God is in control. It is a voice *from the altar* that calls out for the release of these four angels of judgement (9:13); they and their troops therefore come in response to the sovereign will of God. All things are under his control.

### 3. God's severe mercies

At first reading, these chapters do not read like a description of God's mercies. But we must notice, firstly, those who are sealed by God are never harmed (9:4). When the locusts come down and are given power like scorpions, they are told not to harm the grass of the earth or any plant or tree, but only those people who do not have the seal of God on their forehead. Now, what is it to be sealed by God?

Some Christians believe that the seal of the Spirit (Ephesians 1:13) is an experience that only some of God's people have. But the texts that speak of 'sealing' just will not allow this, as we saw in the last chapter. *All* of God's people are sealed; God's 'mark of ownership' is on them all.

This is tremendously important! If there were two classes of Christians—those who had a deep seal of the Spirit and those who were 'merely' born again—then the 'merely' born again would have to suffer all these dreadful tortures in Revelation 9. Only those with the deeper experience would be protected. But that is not what John means. John is saying 'These judgements of God will fall, but they will not touch those who have trusted in Christ.' Those who trust in Christ may well suffer many many things. It is not always easy being a Christian; we do not promise 'Come to Jesus and you will never have another problem.' That is nonsense! But Christians will never taste the judgement of God. These vicious locusts, when they come to you and see the seal of God on your forehead, will pass over. They cannot touch you.

That is the second thing we need to say about the mercy of God in this chapter: that strict limits are set on these judgements. I drew attention earlier to the repeated 'third' in 8:7–12. It occurs twice more in 9:15,18. 'Third' is a large proportion, but it is never the majority and God sets the limit even on these horrendous judgements. The great lesson of the book of Job is that even when Satan moves viciously, his power is always delegated—he can never go any further than God allows him to go. He cannot take one step beyond the purpose of God. That lesson is repeated here. Christian friends, whatever you are feeling, whatever you have been through—today, this week, this year or in the whole of your life—Satan has not been allowed one step beyond what God has allowed for your ultimate good. Though life is often a struggle, the realisation that Satan cannot do anything that our blood-stained and reigning Saviour does not allow is a great comfort. Though Satan has real power and though there is a vicious horde behind him, God sets the limits for them all. There is mercy there, too.

When we worry about evil in the world, when we look at the disasters that happen on our TV screens and say 'Lord, what are you doing?' we do need to ask ourselves, 'What would this world be like if God had removed the restraints?' If there were no Holy Spirit, if there were no Christian people to bear testimony, if there were no law of God in our consciences to cause us to act for the sake of others—if God had removed all those restraints—how much worse would the world be?

## 4. God's 'failed' warnings

These dreadful judgements are real enough judgements, but at the same time they are warnings. You may have noticed how many of them reflect the plagues of Egypt that we read about in the book of Exodus (chapters 7–12). Those plagues too were given in response to the cries of God's people. They were suffering under an Egyptian king that 'did not know about Joseph' (Exodus 1:8). They cried out to God for help and God sent them Moses. In God's name, Moses confronted Pharaoh with the demand that he let the people of Israel go, but Pharaoh refused to listen. As a result, God sent plague after plague—ten plagues in all. All of them were designed to punish Pharaoh for his disobedience and persuade him to let Israel go. Those plagues are mirrored here, and in particular the locusts, the darkness and the blood. Those plagues were warnings, too: warnings to Pharaoh not to think he could triumph over the living God. Again and again Moses said 'if you do this Pharaoh, God will move in judgement!' Again and again Pharaoh backed down in the face of the power of God; but again and again Pharaoh changed his mind. He ignored the warnings of God until eventually the angel of death swept through the land. That was the tenth plague, and every Egyptian household lost its first-born son. Though Pharaoh gave in at this point and let the people go, even then (although it was too late) Pharaoh changed his mind again. This time, his whole pursuing army perished; Pharaoh paid no heed to God's gracious warnings, and he suffered the consequences.

The plagues of Revelation too—these dreadful judgements—are warnings. They are warnings from a God of love: again, and again and again those who attack God's people are destroyed. Sometimes even from our earth-bound perspective we can see it in remarkable ways. To illustrate, let me tell you a true story, while admitting that such stories are the exception not the rule. It is nevertheless a remarkable example of how God can work.

On one occasion we had as a guest a man who had spent much of his adult life in a Soviet prison for his faith. He told us of a Christian friend in prison with him who had escaped. But he had been seen escaping. Two guards had gone after him, and he had not got very far before they caught him. Knocking him to the floor, they raised their clubs to club him—probably to death—knowing that the authorities would not care. Astonishingly, both those men had heart attacks and died at the same moment, the very moment before the first of their blows fell. I have no idea what the chances against that would be. But I do know that those who saw it and those who spoke of it were in awe of the judgement of God. Such a story may be comparatively rare, but it is a vivid illustration for us of the point of these chapters: those who touch God's chosen people will reap their reward. Again and again and again ungodliness reaps its own reward as again and again the wrath of God is revealed from heaven. Warning upon warning upon warning falls on our world.

Yet they are warnings that fail. 'The rest of mankind that were not killed by these plagues still did not repent of the work of their hands (9:20). Is that not an amazing thing? But does it not ring so true? Whatever God does, it seems, people carry on in their own sweet way. They do not repent. They do not stop worshipping demons and idols of gold; they do not repent of their murders, their magic arts, their sexual immorality or their thefts. That is true today. Idolatry is still rife (whatever takes the place of God is an idol—wealth, leisure, family or the gods of other religions). But in spite of the judgements of God, the people of the earth do not repent.

Idolatry smashes 'the first table of the law'—those first four commandments which deal with our relationship to God. But the second table of the Law—to do with our behaviour towards one another—is still flouted too. People murder, they practise magic arts, they are immoral, they steal (9:21). Whatever God does in warning, the commandments are flouted openly. It makes no difference; life and property are not held sacred, covenants are broken. Then judgements fall, and people do not repent.

That is where we come to as we close this chapter. (Notice, we have not yet reached the seventh trumpet. Be patient; we will get there.) Let me press on you that if you are not converted as you read this, the follies of this chapter are your follies! This is your stupidity. Perhaps you can think of times when you have known that you had heard the warning voice of God and seen his judgements fall. But still—ten years, twenty years, fifty years later—you have not come to Christ. Still you carry on without God and without his mercy. Is it rude to suggest this is stupidity? Is it not rather more than stupidity? If you are not God's at this moment, how urgent the need for repentance is. Repentance is not a cheap penny-price you pay to get into heaven and then carry on living in sin. It means surrendering control of your life. It means saying to God, 'Everything about the way I have lived is wrong; from now on it is all under your control. What I do at work, the way I spend my leisure time, the way I run my family life, the place I give to church and Christian work—all that now changes.' That is what repentance is. It is a deep, deep work—and that is what you need if you are not yet converted. Turn to God and he will have mercy on you. These judgements are the severe mercies of God, and they are reluctant judgements. The God and Father of our Lord Jesus Christ is a God who visits judgement on those who refuse him, but he is not a God who delights to do it. We know that because our Lord Jesus Christ stood overlooking Jerusalem, seeing in his mind's eye the dreadful calamity that was about to fall on it (its destruction by the Romans in 70 AD), and he wept for Jerusalem because he loved Jerusalem. He had warned Jerusalem of the dangers of rejecting him, and still it refused him. Some forty years later, God brought judgement on that city. He did not do it because he enjoyed it; he did it for his honour, for his glory, for his righteousness. God's judgements are always reluctant judgements, and we can therefore say with all honesty that if you turn to him he will have mercy on you. The Bible tells us that we must turn to God in repentance and have faith in our Lord Jesus (Acts 20:21). That means turning away from sin and putting our trust in the cross of Christ, who is the sacrifice who bore God's ultimate judgement in our place. If you do that, you will receive the seal of God and God's judgements will never touch you. Nothing—ultimately—in heaven, earth or under the earth—can harm you. When the devouring locusts of devastation see you, they will pass over. Satan can tempt the true believer, and he does. But he can never reclaim those who put their trust in Christ. God's warnings failed; oh that they would not fail with us! Oh that we would know, by his mercy, what it is to call on him, and find deliverance.

**Notes**

1  **William Hendricksen,** *More than conquerors* (Leicester:IVP, 1973), p. 121

# The mystery of God—and the triumph of Satan?

Please read Revelation chapters 10 and 11

D o you want to know when the Lord Jesus Christ is going to return? We know he is going to come again, this time in glory not in humility and suffering. We know that he will return in glory and with his Father's angels, (Matthew 16:27). We know he is going to descend from heaven with a loud command (1 Thessalonians 4:16); we know that the dead in Christ will rise first and we who are left will be caught up with them to meet him in the air (1 Thessalonians 4:17). But would you like to know when?

Scripture discourages speculation about the date, and the Lord Jesus says 'It is not for you to know the times or the dates the Father has set by his own authority,'(Acts 1:7). But still—without wanting to know what God has chosen to keep to himself—a hint would be nice, would it not? After all, though he is coming like a thief in the night—that is, without sending warning—it does seem that in the New Testament that this phrase (which is used twice: Matthew 24:43, 1 Thessalonians 5:2) is spoken of unbelievers, not believers. He has given *us* a warning—about the reality of it, at least. Has he also said anything about the timing of it?

I believe he may have. Not that he has told us the month and day, nor even the year. But God has certainly told us what to watch for, and may have given us at least a pointer to the general time. That hint is in this passage, and we will get to it in this chapter.

## Arm of the Lord, awake!
In our last chapter, we noted that Revelation 8–11 forms one section in the book, a section that is about God answering the cries of his people. As the saints in heaven cry out 'How long?' (6:10), so the saints on earth cry out in their suffering. Their prayers are mingled with the intercession of Christ on

their behalf (8:3). Their prayers reach the ears of God, and in response the judgements of God fall on the persecuting people; and they are terrible judgements. We began to see, then, how awesome a weapon prayer can be. So it is appropriate sometimes to sing:

Arm of the Lord awake awake!
Thy power unconquerable take;
Thy strength put on, assert thy might,
And triumph in the dreadful fight.

Haste then but come not to destroy,
Mercy is thine, thy crown, thy joy ...

(Henry March, 1791–1869)

as we call on God to answer our prayers. We do want him to deliver us; but knowing the terror of the Lord, we want him to deliver us and at the same time show mercy to his enemies by bringing them to repentance.

These judgements are so terrible that when they fall, men seek death but cannot find it; they long to die but death eludes them (9:6); as the Scripture says, it is a dreadful thing to fall into the hands of the Living God (Hebrews 10:31). Those who mock his word, mock his name, or mock his day; those who make sport of his church and laugh at the worship of the Living God need to understand that this is no joke. It is a fearsome thing to taunt God in that way! In particular, it is a fearful thing to attack the anointed of the Lord, the Church of the Lord Jesus.

We saw too that Christians are those who have been sealed by the Lord (9:4), and they are not touched by those judgements. God's judgements never fall on his people. God certainly *disciplines* his people, but he never visits them with judgement. So, what is happening to the church while the judgements of chapters 8 and 9 are falling on the world? That is what this vision turns to next. In one sense, we have seen it already in earlier chapters; now we see it from a new perspective. These chapters are very full; you will find it helpful to have your Bibles open as we proceed.

## Another angle

Let us begin then in chapter 10, with the angel and the scroll. 'Then I saw another mighty angel coming down from heaven. He was robed in a cloud, with a rainbow above his head; his face was like the sun, and his legs were like fiery pillars. He was holding a little scroll, which lay open in his hand. He planted his right foot on the sea and his left foot on the land …' (10:1–2). We see a mighty angel and we hear a mysterious announcement.

In some respects, this angel in chapter 10 sounds rather like the Lord Jesus Christ; his face is like the Sun, his legs are fiery pillars, he is robed in a cloud and has a rainbow above his head. All of this sounds rather like the description of the Lord Jesus in chapter one. He speaks and it is the voice of seven thunders (verse 3), and Psalm 29 compares the voice of God to thunder. Then we are told that his angel plants his right foot on the sea and his left foot on the land, showing the awesome power of Jesus, for God has put everything under his feet. Hence some commentators are quite sure that this is Jesus; this angel is the angel of the Lord, the angel of Jehovah, Jesus himself.

But I think not; for a number of reasons. Firstly, the angel swears by him who lives for ever and ever (verse 6); and that is not an oath that God himself takes. When God swears an oath, he swears by himself (Hebrews 6:13–14) because there is no-one greater for him to swear by. Secondly, a voice comes from heaven in verse 8 and commands John to take the scroll from the hand of the angel. We are told that it is the voice he has heard before: that is, this voice is the voice of Jesus. So the angel cannot be Jesus. Thirdly, John does not fall down and worship this angel, as he worships the Lord Jesus in chapter one, and finally, it is doubtful whether Revelation ever refers to Jesus as an angel.

Yet because his description does sound like a description of Christ, at the very least this angel must be a high and glorious representative, and he is a creature of awesome power.

## No more time?

When this angel speaks, it is the voice of seven thunders and the message is awesome (3–4). Naturally, John wants to write down what those seven thunders have said. But he is commanded not to; like Paul (2 Corinthians 12:4), John has heard things that he is not permitted to describe. These things must be sealed up, not written down.

John does tell us though the angel's next words: 'There will be no more delay.' That is the best translation: not 'there will be no more time,' as the AV has it. Some ancient philosophers have insisted that there could be no time in heaven or the after-life. Many Christians have taken that view as if it were a Biblical doctrine and found support for it in this verse. But it is unnecessary and unlikely; we cannot conceive of events at all—and certainly not sequences of events—without time. The whole idea of 'sequence' becomes meaningless if there is no time. And we have no grounds at all for thinking that there is no time in heaven; it is not what the angel is saying here.

The word in the Greek is 'chronos' (from which we get 'chronological') and 'time' is its normal meaning; but it can mean delay or time in the sense of seasons. The declaration of the angel is that there will be no more seasons to come, no more delay. For in the day when the seventh angel is about to sound his trumpet, the mystery of God will be accomplished.

## The mystery of God

What then is the mystery of God? 'The mystery of God will be accomplished,' it says, 'just as he announced to his servants the prophets.' What does it mean?

We will find a clue in Romans 16:25–27: 'Now to him who is able to establish you by my gospel and the proclamation of Jesus Christ, according to the revelation of *the mystery hidden for long ages past*, but now revealed and made known through the prophetic writings by the command of the eternal God, so that all nations might believe and obey him—to the only wise God be glory forever through Jesus Christ! Amen.' 'Mystery' then, for Paul at least, refers to something that has been hidden for long ages past but is made known through the prophetic writings so that all nations might believe and obey him. How do all nations come to believe and obey God? Only through the gospel. 'All nations' is a concept taken up in Revelation 10 as well, as John must prophesy again (vs. 11) 'about many peoples, nations, languages and kings.' So for both Paul (in Romans) and John (in Revelation), the mystery of God is the message that is to go out from the apostles to all the world, that is, it is the gospel itself!

When the Bible uses the word 'mystery', it is in a different sense than our normal use. For us, a mystery may be a book telling a story but only revealing 'who done it' on the last page. For Biblical writers however, 'mystery' is something that had been hidden but has now been revealed. The gospel had been proclaimed, certainly, through the prophets and their writings but only now has it been made known and opened up so that people from all nations will believe and obey. A glance at how the word is used in Ephesians will help us understand it further.

Ephesians 1:9–10 reads 'And he made known to us the mystery of his will according to his good pleasure, which he purposed in Christ, to be put into effect when the times will have reached their fulfilment—to bring all things in heaven and on earth together under one head, even Christ.' The 'mystery' here is described as God's purpose to reconcile all things together in Christ. We certainly cannot say yet about the world we live in that all things have been reconciled together! There is a great deal of enmity in the world itself, and a great deal of enmity too with God. God and his world have, as it were, been wrenched apart by sin; there is an enormous distance between them. But the day is coming when all things will be reconciled to God, reconciled in the gospel of Christ. It is not just human beings, but the very heavens and the earth—all of creation—which is going to be brought together, renewed under one head, even Christ. As Paul writes in Romans, 'the creation itself will be liberated from its bondage to decay and brought into the glorious freedom of the children of God' (8:21).

The 'mystery' here then—something once hidden but now made known—is God's purpose to make the man Christ Jesus, through the gospel, the head of all creation—and a new, reconciled creation at that.

## Key to the Scriptures

If any one verse could be said to be a key to all the Scriptures—which would be a bold thing to say about any verse—I believe that the verse would be Philippians 2:10: 'that at the name of Jesus every knee should bow, in heaven and on earth and under the earth.' Every knee: nothing less suits the purpose of God. Of course, it is true that not every knee will bow willingly; not everyone will be saved. But the gospel reveals, more plainly than ever before, that it has always been God's purpose to save Gentiles as well as Jews; hence Paul says in Ephesians 3:6 'this mystery is that through the gospel the Gentiles are heirs together with Israel, members together of one body, and sharers together in the promise in Christ Jesus.'

Mistakenly, some Christians believe that the inclusion of Gentiles in God's saving purposes is a kind of afterthought in the mind of God. The Old Testament, they tell us, speaks of the nation of Israel, and Israel is not and never was a part of the church. Only when Israel rejected their Messiah did God decide to include the Gentiles in his mercy.

But John's words in Revelation, and Paul's words in Ephesians, show us how mistaken this is. The prophets spoke the word of God to the people of Israel, calling them back to God in repentance. But right from the book of Genesis (18:18, for example), the prophets also spoke, in relatively veiled terms, of a day when all the nations of the earth will be blessed by the God of Israel. This is seen again and again in the prophets. For example, Isaiah tells us that Christ's blood (representing, of course, God's salvation) will 'sprinkle many nations' (52:15). Amos prophesies of Gentile nations seeking the Lord (9:11–12: quoted in Acts 15:16ff), and the Scriptures could easily be multiplied. The writers of the Old Testament knew that their God was not a tribal God, limited to one nation and one people. Rather, they saw that the day is coming when all the earth will acknowledge him. The gospel is God's way of accomplishing that; he spreads the glory of his name as preachers go throughout the world—we will see more about that in a moment.

Tragically though as he spreads the glory of his name in the world by the gospel, there are many who continue to oppose him, many who refuse Jesus. Yet from every nation and tongue and tribe and people there are people who hear the good news, respond to it and are made one people together in Christ. Jew, Gentile, pagan, Barbarian, Scythian, bond, free, male female—all are one in Christ Jesus. And as we have seen, that is not the end; the day is coming when all the creation will be regenerated—made new—and put under the head, under Christ, under that man that suffered and died for our sake. Because of his obedience he has been highly exalted to the place which is above every place and given the name that is above every name.

In the days when the seventh angel is about to sound his trumpet, says John, the mystery of God will be accomplished—that is, it will be completed. There will be no more delay. To put it another way, the gospel age—the age in which we live—is the last age; it is the last dispensation. There is no other age and no other dispensation to come.

Why is this important? It is particularly important today with the rise of Islam. Islam teaches that Jesus was indeed a great prophet of Allah, but that there was a greater prophet to come (Mohammed) and that the age of Christianity must pass and the age of Islam must rise. But sincere as our Muslim friends undoubtedly are, this is false. There is no more delay; when the mystery of God has been accomplished through the gospel, and God has gathered together in Christ all his people, then the last trumpet will sound. To give another example: the Bahai faith (which itself sprung from Islam) teaches that all religions have their springtime but they fade into winter, and then God has to do a new thing. Christianity was once the new thing; then Islam, but now Bahai is the new religion for this age. But again, it is false; there are no more delays and no more ages. Jesus is the King; Jesus is the Saviour. The gospel age is the last age.

## The bitter-sweet scroll

'Then the voice that I had heard from heaven spoke to me once more.' This is our Lord Jesus Christ. Since he speaks from heaven and commands John to go to the angel 'who is standing on the sea and on the land', we have added evidence that this angel is not Jesus. The voice says '"Go, take the scroll that lies open in the hand of the angel who is standing on the sea and on the land." So I went to the angel and asked him to give me the little scroll. He said to me, 'Take it and eat it. It will turn your stomach sour, but in your mouth it will be as sweet as honey"' (10:8–9).

To understand Revelation properly, we need to be very familiar with the Old Testament. A good cross reference Bible is invaluable, too: cross references here will certainly help us understand the passage that we are reading. We will certainly be pointed to Jeremiah 15.16 where Jeremiah is told to eat God's words, and he ate them and said that they were his joy and his heart's delight. After that, cross references will then point us to Ezekiel where he is told (2:10–3:14) to eat a scroll with words of mourning and lament and woe on the scroll. Ezekiel said it was as sweet as honey in his mouth, but when he goes out to proclaim the words ingested, he goes in bitterness to proclaim them.

So, back to Revelation 10, where verses 9–11 speak of the work of John and the work of every gospel preacher. In fact, what they say is true of every one who ever proclaims the gospel, whether publicly or in private conversation; John here represents the whole church. John is to prophesy; he is to speak out. What he is to speak out is a gospel which is both sweet and sour. It is sweet in our mouths, we are told. That is the gospel, certainly; we have heard it and we have come to love it. Though we have many faults and failings, and many sins, the truth about every Christian is that we love this gospel so much we would not trade *anything* for it and we would not trade *everything* for it; it is sweet to us. Because we love the gospel, it is so very sweet when the gospel is in our mouths—that is, it is a real joy to tell others about the Lord Jesus. But at the same time, when we begin to proclaim it, what a burden it can be. We ache for those who reject it; they are so unwilling to listen, and they show so little interest. Inevitably, it grieves us because we know where their indifference will lead them—unless they repent. Then, too, preaching this gospel often produces persecution, and it brings a different sort of pain. When people who have hitherto been relatively harmless are stirred up to oppose God and his gospel, then it becomes like sourness in our stomachs. Yet still—sweet to the taste, sour in the stomach—this scroll, book and gospel must be proclaimed.

### The temple, two witnesses, and the time of the end

Chapter 11 typifies gospel preaching again, this time by introducing us to two witnesses. Before we meet them, though, we must consider the temple.

John is told to measure the temple (11:1) and given 'a reed like a measuring rod' to do this. Plainly, this is not the physical temple in Jerusalem; if Revelation was written around AD90, as we think, that temple has been destroyed for twenty years or so. But the temple represents the true people of God; they are the temple of God, (1 Corinthians 3:16, Ephesians 2:21). Though we are told here that the temple is to be measured, not until much later are we given the measurements. What does this 'measuring' mean?

Some refer it back to Ezekiel 40–48. There, too, the temple is measured, and it seems to represent God's safekeeping of the temple, in spite of the apparent victory of his enemies. So the 'measuring' here, like the 'sealing' in previous chapters, would be a sign that God will keep his people. It is certainly a promise that needs repeating; for throughout the whole period that the church is proclaiming its message ('prophesying', 11:3) the temple (the people of God) are being trampled on (11:2). Proclamation and persecution go hand-in-hand throughout the whole period.

But here in these verses is, perhaps, hidden a mystery in our ordinary use of that word. Here perhaps is a hint—just a hint—as to when the return of our Lord Jesus Christ will be. While this temple does represent the true people of God in all times, there is a reference too to the Holy City, Jerusalem. It would not be unusual in the New Testament for prophecy about the fate of Jerusalem to be mingled with a prophecy about the end of the world: see, for example, Matthew 24. We will work out the possible implications of this in a moment.

Meanwhile, the Gentiles, we are told, are to trample on the Holy City for forty-two months. If the Jews represent the people of God, the Gentiles represent his enemies. Forty-two months is three and a half years; if each month has thirty days—an idealised month—then forty-two months is one thousand two hundred and sixty days. We will see more references to that period in Revelation; this is the first of them. This period was first mentioned in Daniel (time, times and half a time, 7:25, see Revelation 12:14) as the period during which the saints would be persecuted.

The Gentiles are to trample on the Holy City for three and a half years. That means they are going to persecute the true people of God—the 'temple'. As I have said, it may also be a reference to something else; we will return to that.

First, let us look at the two witnesses. Who are they? 'I will give power to my two witnesses. They will prophesy for one thousand, two hundred and sixty days... These are the two olive trees and the two lampstands that stand before the Lord of the earth. If anyone tries to harm them, fire comes from their mouths and devours their enemies. This is how anyone who wants to harm them must die. These men have power to shut up the sky so that it will not rain during the time they are prophesying; and they have power to turn the waters into blood' (11:4–6.). Once more, one thousand, two hundred and sixty days is mentioned; the same length of time. The witnesses sound rather like Elijah and Moses—Elijah who called down fire on Mount Carmel to destroy God's enemies, and who shut up the heavens so that it did not rain until he said so; and Moses who turned the waters into blood and struck the earth with plague. Some people then, taking Revelation rather more literally than I think is warranted, interpret this as meaning that the time will come when Elijah and Moses will return to earth. They will point out that Elijah never died, and they may try to argue too that neither did Moses (though we are told that he was buried by God himself and only God knows where his grave is: Deuteronomy 34:5–6).

It seems to me as unnecessary, fanciful and extremely unlikely that we are meant to take these figures so literally. As we have seen already so many times, Revelation is a symbolic book, and everyone takes it as symbolic at some point.

The best way of taking this is to look in the Old Testament for the key to two witnesses, without literalising these two characters. Two is the number of testimony—a report by two witnesses is to be believed: 'A matter must be established by the testimony of two or three witnesses' (Deuteronomy 19:15). Here in Revelation 11 then, God is saying that there will be a faithful testimony throughout this whole period of forty-two months. That period symbolically represents the whole gospel age. The two witnesses then represent the whole church, and they prophesy the word of God for the whole of that period. It is a limited period, not for ever: a symbolic three and a half years. The symbolic interpretation is strengthened when we realise that the imagery of the olive trees and lampstands here comes from Zechariah 4, where there is one lampstand and two olive trees. Lampstands in Revelation represent the church (see Revelation 1), and olive trees seem to have the same meaning in the Old Testament, especially perhaps in the book of Psalms.

Now, if there is a mingling of prophecy about the earthly city of Jerusalem with prophecy about the end times, this is where the hint about the time of the end might be. The Gentiles are to trample the Holy City for forty-two months, the whole gospel age. It is at least possible that this is the same period that our Lord Jesus Christ describes in Luke 21:24 as 'the times of the Gentiles': 'Jerusalem will be trampled on by the Gentiles until the times of the Gentiles are fulfilled.' If that is right, then not only is the gospel persecuted to the very end, but the earthly city of Jerusalem is also occupied by Gentiles to the very end. But the Gentiles occupied Jerusalem, we know—the literal, physical Jerusalem—from AD70 until 1966. So it may well be (and that is as dogmatic as I am prepared to be, now or ever!) that we have come to the end of the times of the Gentiles already; the gospel age may be drawing to a close. That may be the reason why we are seeing, in our own days, many more Jewish people converted. The times of the Gentiles are past, there is a beginning of a work among the Jews, working towards the latter-day revival in Israel that Romans 11 describes. This whole subject is shrouded in mystery, and the only thing we can be sure of is that anyone who is too dogmatic is likely to be dogmatically wrong! But this would certainly make our own day an enormously exciting time.

Now let us return to the two witnesses. They have fire coming from their mouths, destroying their foes. Those who will attack God's people must suffer. It is a fearful thing to fall into the hands of the living God. Then as these witnesses come to the end of their testimony, a beast comes from the abyss (verse 7). This abyss is the very pit of hell, and the beast attacks the witnesses, overpowering and killing them. Their bodies are left to lie in the streets—the streets of Jerusalem 'figuratively called Sodom and Egypt, where also their Lord was crucified.' These three places represent the world in its great opposition to God; Sodom was the place of enormous sexual sin, destroyed by God in judgement; Egypt is the nation that held God's people in captivity; Jerusalem—which should have been the capital of godliness—has joined Sodom and Egypt in its contempt for God by crucifying his Son. For three and a half days there is great rejoicing as people from all over the world gaze on their bodies, refuse to bury them, send one another celebratory gifts. What does this mean?

The proclamation of the gospel has—at the very least—gone into decline. The witness of the church has been effectively silenced—but only for a short period, and a period which God chooses (since their testimony was 'finished'). The church, it seems, is eclipsed for a little while. It is dead—though not forever; like its Lord, it will be resurrected.

A little knowledge of history will tell us that this is just what has happened down the ages. The gospel spread rapidly in the time of the apostles. In fact it spread through the whole world in their lifetime, so that the apostle Paul was able to talk about all the world having heard

(Colossians 1:6). But after a while it went into eclipse; we still speak about the 'Dark Ages,' a period when the church continued but the gospel was all but forgotten. In spite of the existence of a formal church on the earth, it seems that barely one in a thousand of its adherents and ministers really knew what the gospel was. It almost seems as if Christians had been destroyed; their witness was silenced. Whenever that happens, the whole world is glad. These troublesome believers have finally been silenced! Now the world can get on with doing what it wants! For centuries the church has been telling the world how to live, passing their laws and limiting the world's freedoms; now they're gone! 'Let us eat and drink and be merry,' says the world, (forgetting that 'tomorrow we die'). 'Let us celebrate!'

But their joy is premature, for after only a very short period (represented by three and a half days: not three and a half years, this time) a breath of life from God enters the witnesses. They stand on their feet again and terror strikes those who saw them. When the church goes into eclipse it can only ever be a temporary eclipse, and then the Spirit of God will blow again on the world. The testimony of God's people will be revived, for Jesus has said 'I will build my church, and the gates of Hades will not overcome it' (Matthew 16:18). When for a little while it seems that the gates of hell have triumphed, and God's church is destroyed, it will always be premature to write its obituary! On the contrary, let those who hate God and his gospel tremble; the day will surely come when the breath of heaven will blow again on the church and it will live. Let us take a definite example.

In the Spring of 1514, a report was made to the Pope that there were no more heretics in Europe—'heretic' being at that time Roman Catholic 'code' for Bible-believers. They had been silenced and the 'church' could rest easy. But in October 1517, almost exactly (as it happens) three and a half years later, Luther nailed his 95 theses to the door of the church in Wittenberg and the Great Reformation began. The Reformation was a mighty explosion of Biblical understanding and a great return to true Christianity from the corrupt mixture that is Roman Catholicism. The 'heretics' were back—and in greater force than ever before! When some early Reformation scholars noticed that three and a half year period, and read of this three and a half days in Revelation, they linked it with Ezekiel's principle (Ezekiel 4:6) of 'a day for each year'. Inevitably perhaps, they saw these three and a half days as prophesying those three and a half years, and so were sure that the Great Reformation meant that this particular period in Revelation had now been reached.

Of course, they were absolutely right—although they were a little bit wrong, as well! They were absolutely right because that was precisely what was happening. When the enemies of the gospel were saying 'It's all over; we've destroyed them at last! We can enjoy ourselves now!' then God breathed his Spirit. He did not breathe on Rome, the centre of the church's power. Instead, he breathed in Germany. He did not breathe on a bishop in all his power and apparent influence, but on an obscure monk. God said, 'Let my people live' and a fire of truth was lit which still burns throughout the world. Those early Reformers may have been wrong in thinking it was *the* fulfilment of this prophecy (I think they were), but they were certainly right in seeing that it was *a* fulfilment. The gospel does know periods of decline; the western world is in the midst of one of those periods now. For all the apparent growth in the professed church in Britain over the last twenty years, there are still signs of decline on every hand. Enemies of the church rejoice on every hand, as every vestige of Biblical morality is shrugged off. But once again, the rejoicing is premature; God has only to breathe his Spirit and we will live again.

Greater declines may yet come. It may well be, as many Christians believe, that before the end of the age—before the Lord Jesus Christ returns—there will be a great apostasy, a greater period of decline than we have ever known in history. Perhaps it will be a period when it seems even the churches themselves have abandoned the faith. But if and when such a period comes—a period when Satan seems to have triumphed—we need to remember that his apparent triumphs are never real.

The ultimate picture of that of course is the cross. For thirty years, Satan had tried to destroy God's Messiah. He moved Herod against Jesus when he was a baby, but failed to destroy the child. Satan whipped up a storm, attempting to drown the Lord Jesus at the beginning of his ministry (Mark 4:35–41), but only succeeded in revealing Jesus' power. He took the Lord on in a face-to-face contest in the wilderness, attempting to persuade Jesus to abandon his mission and worship Satan, but again he failed. Then came the cross of Calvary, where Satan thought he had finally succeeded. The

Messiah was dead! How all the hordes of Satan must have rejoiced! But not for very long; in fact, for a little less than a literal three and a half days. Then Jesus burst from the tomb, and the doom of Satan was accomplished! The cross did not mark the triumph of Satan, but his defeat.

That is the way it always is, and it is the way it is here in Revelation 11. The breath of God breathes on the church, and the church rises again. Terror strikes those who see the renewed life of the church and a voice comes from heaven saying 'Come up here,' and the witnesses are taken to heaven. This is not a reference to the end, when all God's people are taken up to heaven in a cloud. Rather, it indicates that they are knowing the blessing of God in a way which no-one can deny. Not only is the church revived, she is caught up by God—and then, certainly at the last, will be caught up in the clouds to be with her Lord for ever and ever. Whether or not there is one final, massive eclipse for the gospel may be debatable; but there is certainly a final triumph! The triumph of Satan is always short-lived. (Incidentally, verse 12b 'Come up here' does not refer to a secret rapture. Their enemies are watching and see what happens; whatever else, this is not secret.)

Finally, we come to the time of the seventh trumpet. The second woe spoke of the silencing of the church's witness, and it has passed. The third woe to come on the earth is the final judgement. John introduces it here without describing it; he will describe it later, and we will see it in a later chapter. Let us now just notice, firstly, that the reign of Christ is acknowledged. 'The kingdom of the world has become the kingdom of our Lord and of his Christ' (Revelation 11:15). Second, his reign is eternal: 'and he will reign for ever and ever.' Thirdly, his reign is a praiseworthy reign: 'We give thanks to you, Lord God Almighty, the One who is and who was, because you have taken your great power and have begun to reign' (11:17). But still, the reign of Christ is also a dreadful thing for those who have opposed him: 'The nations were angry; and your wrath has come. The time has come for judging the dead' (11:18). What a time that will be! It is also a rewarding reign: the time has come for 'rewarding your servants the prophets and your saints and those who reverence your name, both small and great' (11:18b).

Verse 19 shows a temple in heaven opened. There in the temple is the Ark of the Covenant, surrounded by flashes of lightning and rumblings and peals of thunder, an earthquake and great hailstorms. It is an awesome thing, because the Ark of the Covenant symbolises the place where God dwells. But the Ark also symbolises fellowship between God and man, because the lid of that Ark is the mercy-seat, and it is a blood-stained thing. The Ark symbolises perfect fellowship between God and man on the basis of shed blood. On that day of judgement, that shed blood will have its power revealed more completely than ever before. Its power will be demonstrated in heaven, so that all those who fear the name of God, all those who are bought by the blood, all who have worshipped the Lord, whether they are small or great, receive their reward. We need to remember that phrase, 'small and great'. The certain fact is our Lord Jesus Christ reigns, and he will triumph. To live for Christ is hard, and the world is against us. Yet even in this life, the Evil One has less power over us than over the world; in a very real sense—and we will see this spelled out again in coming chapters—nothing Satan does can harm us. Our Lord Jesus Christ said 'Do not be afraid of those who kill the body but cannot kill the soul. Rather, be afraid of the One who can destroy both soul and body in hell' (Matthew 10:28). For the non-Christian, that is an astonishing thing. 'Do not be afraid of those who can only kill you,' he says. 'What else is there?' says the unbeliever. 'Oh,' says the Lord Jesus, 'There is one who can destroy both soul and body in hell. Be afraid of him.' And Christian people are those who are afraid; but not of death. They are afraid only of sin, and its damnation. They know that once they are delivered from that, Satan can do nothing to harm them. Nothing. (We must return to this in the next chapter.)

Sometimes our experience seems to contradict this. 'Satan has had a pretty good go at me this week,' we might be tempted to say. Perhaps he has; but if so, it was with the permission of the Lord Jesus Christ—and Satan has not hurt us, because he cannot hurt us. We are safe in the hands of the Lord, and the day is coming when all who reverence his name will be rewarded. So we press on, hard though it may be, for the reward—like Jesus, 'who for the joy set before him endured the cross, scorning its shame' (Hebrews 12:2)—so we despise the shame of the world for the joy that is set before us in Christ, for the reward and the sight of the Saviour.

'Jesus, Jesus, all sufficient,
Beyond telling is thy worth.
In thy name lie greater treasures
Than the richest found on earth.
Such abundance
Is my portion with my God.

(William Williams, translated by RM Jones)

All the trials and sacrifices and perils and pains of earth, all—all—are worth paying for one glimpse of the face of the Saviour. Not one of us will ever be forgotten. Those we call 'great saints', and those who seem to be 'small saints' are all remembered and rewarded by the Lord Jesus. CH Spurgeon was one of the great ones—in our estimation. He ministered to thousands for nearly half a century, and his works still encircle the globe. Sixty-three volumes of his sermons are still available, and now even on one CD-ROM. By the blessing of God, the truth that man proclaimed will go on down the ages being an enormous blessing to the church of God. Though Spurgeon died in 1892, I know men younger than I who were converted through his (printed) ministry. What a man he was, and what a ministry! But all through the world, and all down the ages, there are tens of thousands of people that we think of as less important Christians. Pastors in small flocks; Sunday School teachers; youth workers; local preachers and the like. They are men and women whose names are not only never known by the world, they are never even known by the church at large. But they are people who bear testimony for Jesus to their neighbour, to the children in their charge—people who do what they can out of reverence for the Lord. Neither Spurgeon nor these little ones will be overlooked by the Lord Jesus Christ. All those who reverence his name will be rewarded, both small and great. So shall we, if we are among them. For we will never be the great ones of the world nor the great ones of the church. But it does not matter. For the day is coming when all who reverence him—yes, even that child who once, in her class, stood up to the teacher who was ridiculing her Saviour—even that little one will not be forgotten, and will get her reward. He does not overlook anyone. The kingdom of the world is become the kingdom of our Lord and of his Christ; and he will reign for ever.

*And he shall reign for ever,*
*His throne and crown shall ever endure.*
*And he shall reign for ever,*
*And we shall reign with him.*

What a vision filled my eyes,
One like a Son of man.
Coming with the clouds of heav'n
He approached an awesome throne.

He was given sovereign power,
Glory and authority.
Every nation, tribe and tongue
Worshipped him on bended knee.

*And he shall reign for ever,*
*His throne and crown shall ever endure.*
*And he shall reign for ever,*
*And we shall reign with him.*

On the throne for ever,
See the Lamb who once was slain
Wounds of sacrificial love
Forever shall remain.

(Graham Kendrick. Copyright 1991, Make Way Music.)

# The rage of the red dragon

Please read Revelation 12–14

Iwant to tell you in this chapter the secret of victory over the devil; how to defeat him always, every time, and never fail. I want to give you a little secret which will ensure—if you use it—that Satan will never get the victory over you again. It is an easy secret to learn, and we will come to it later in the chapter.

By now we should have discovered how exciting the Book of Revelation is, and that it is better to be excited by it than afraid of it. We should have learned that God wants us to understand it. It is part of his word and has a message for us. Standing back at a distance and trying to catch the sweep of the book is the best way of grasping the message of the seven parallel visions that make up the book. Each of the visions is complete in itself, and in this chapter we look at the fourth of the seven visions. It is a very important vision, and it introduces characters and concepts that will return later. It is also important because it tells us what is really going on on the earth. One repeated message of Revelation is that it is hard to be a part of the church of Christ in a world that despises him; in this vision we are shown that the difficulties stem from a red dragon who hates God and his people.

## The hatred of the dragon

Chapter 12:1–6 reveals for us the hatred of the dragon. As we approach these verses, remember that there may be several different explanations of the same event which are all true at the same time.

Let me give you an example. Suppose early one morning you had been by the side of the M4 and you had watched my car speed by at seventy miles an hour. If someone had asked you 'Why is Gary driving down this road at seventy miles an hour?' there are various explanations you could have given. If you were committed to a purely mechanical view of the universe, you might have said, 'Well, his foot is on the accelerator and petrol is being ignited which is driving the pistons which are driving the wheels' (or however it is that these things work!) If you knew me very well, you might have said 'He is driving at that speed because he ignored his alarm clock this morning and he has to be in Cardiff for 11 a.m.' If you were very cynical you might have said 'He is driving at that speed because there's a police car not far behind him and he dare not go any faster.' Now these explanations are not mutually exclusive; all three could be right at the same time!

Life is like that. The earlier chapters of Revelation have shown us in symbolic form the sufferings of the church and the judgements that God brings on the world. The church endures her sufferings as a result of the judgements of God. Now, because the visions are parallel, we see the same sweep of events. These chapters describe the same period from the birth of our Lord Jesus Christ right up to his return in glory at the end of the age. This time, though, we see that the sufferings in the world are caused by the devil himself, the red dragon of these chapters. We are seeing more of the spiritual realities behind the events on earth.

Having seen what is happening on the earth, now John has his eyes open to see what is behind these earthly events. The explanation of all the sufferings of the world, and of the church in particular, is the dragon: the hatred of the dragon, the defeat of the dragon and the rage of the dragon. Let us turn to what he sees.

## The hatred of the dragon

If we were to draw the scene that John describes at the beginning of chapter 12, the drawing would be almost pornographic. First, John sees a woman and she is in labour. She is about to give birth and suffering labour pains, and stood ready to catch the child as it is born—standing, as it were, between the feet of this labouring woman—is a red dragon. He is waiting for the birth of the child so that when it arrives, he can eat it. He wants to devour this child.

Who is the woman? Plainly the child is Christ: verse 5 tells us that the woman gave birth to a son who was to rule all the nations with an iron sceptre. This is a direct quote from Psalm 2:9 ('You will rule them with an iron sceptre ; you will dash them to pieces like pottery' ), which is a psalm that speaks of the Lord Jesus. (If you want proof of that, compare verse 7 with Acts 13:33.) So the woman is one who has given birth to the Christ.

The whole of what we might call 'gospel event' is then described in a few words. The child was snatched up to God and his throne: so Christ is born, he lives, he dies, he rises from the dead and he ascends into heaven—it is all there in those few words. But if the child is Christ, who is the woman?

It plainly cannot be speaking about Mary, the mother of Jesus. We know that not just because it is symbolism, but because the woman is taken into the desert (verse 6) where she is cared for during the whole gospel period— one thousand two hundred and sixty days. As we saw in the last chapter, this period—sometimes described as one thousand two hundred and sixty days, sometimes as forty two months, sometimes as three and a half years (time, times and half a time)—represents the whole of the gospel age. But Mary the mother of Jesus does not live that long! So this cannot refer to Mary.

Therefore, there is only one choice: this woman represents the nation of Israel, which 'gave birth' to the Lord Jesus Christ. God worked again and again through the whole history of the Old Testament to keep the nation pure. He sent them prophets to instruct them and rebuke them. When they did not listen, he sent them into captivity when they abandoned him. He used defeat and captivity to bring them back to their senses, to bring them back to repentance and then geographically bring them back to their own land. One purpose of all this, in fact the main purpose, was to keep the nation alive and pure so that the Christ could be born from that nation.

To say that she is the nation of Israel, though, is not the complete picture. After Christ is 'snatched up to God and his throne' the woman flees into the desert for the whole gospel period. There she is pursued by the dragon (verse 13) and protected by God (verse 16) as a result of which the dragon turns his attention to her offspring. Who then is she? She is the people of God, both Israel (in the Old Testament period) from whom Christ is born and the Christian church (in the New Testament period).

Note how glorious this woman is. She is clothed with the Sun, we are told (verse 1). The moon is under her feet, and a crown of twelve stars is on her head. God sees his church—his people in the world—as infinitely glorious. When he describes her to the angels, he does not speak of their sins and faults and failing; he describes her as clothed with the Sun. The church is infinitely glorious, the most beautiful thing on earth to God. The number

12 is symbolic and always, in Revelation, represents the church; and the sun and the moon perhaps underline that she represents the people of God in the two ages, Old Testament and New. For in the New Testament, the people of God are the church of Christ. It is not wrong to call God's people in the Old Testament 'the church' (see Acts 7:38 where 'assembly' in the NIV translates the Greek word 'ecclesia', which is usually translated 'church'). But the church in the Old Testament does not have the glory of the New Testament church; it is only a shadow, only a reflection—just as the Moon has no light of her own, but simply reflects that of the Sun.

Here then is a glorious woman, representing a glorious people, the people of God. From that woman comes the Messiah. Jesus is called 'the seed of the woman' in the very first promise we are given about him (Genesis 3.15),where we are told that the woman will bear a seed and that seed will crush the serpent—this very serpent that is here in the figure of a dragon. The purpose for which the Lord Jesus—the seed of the woman— came into the world was to crush that serpent and destroy his works (see Hebrews 2:14 and 1 John 3:8).

When the child is born, the dragon's purpose to destroy the baby is thwarted. We are not told how, only that he is snatched up to God and his throne. We know of course that Satan literally tried to destroy the baby Jesus; remember the slaughter of the children in Jerusalem by Herod (Matthew 2:16)? There were other times, too, when Satan tried to engineer a premature death for Jesus (for example, in Mark 4:38–41, when a furious storm blows up while Jesus is asleep in the stern). When Jesus did die at last on Calvary, Satan thought that at last he had the victory and had accomplished his purpose—though no-one has ever been more wrong! For Calvary was the great defeat of Satan, after which God takes his Son into heaven, far beyond the reach of Satan forever.

So, this vision tells us, when Satan's purpose to destroy Christ is thwarted, he turns on the woman—now representing the New Testament church. She then has to flee into the desert, where she might be taken care of until Christ returns. She has to trust herself to God's care in a hostile world—the hostile world symbolised so well by the desert or wilderness. The church of Jesus is always a wilderness church.

Whenever we see a church of Christ—so called—wielding great power and pomp and glory—then we need to ask very seriously whether it is a true church of Jesus or not. The true church, we are told here, is in the wilderness. It is a fleeing people. It is not a city nor a kingdom here on earth, and the great wealth and power of some sections of the church only indicate that those sections are not the church at all. When the sixteenth-century Reformers protested against the errors of the Roman Catholic Church, that Church said 'But look at our glory. Look at our power; look at our wealth.' The proper response was 'Quite. But where is the wilderness church?'

Who then is the dragon? He is Satan, the accuser of the brethren. He is a peculiar monster, having seven heads and ten horns. The heads and the horns represent dominion and power in Scripture. Horns always represent strength and power, and ten is the symbol of completeness in the Bible. Thus we are being told that this dragon has dominion and power throughout the whole world. All the kingdoms of this world are under his control, and he exercises that power with a specific purpose: to destroy the child. As we noticed earlier, it is a rather gruesome picture, and when he fails to destroy the child he turns his attention on the church, but she flees to the desert. This is the hatred of the dragon; let us now look at the defeat of the dragon, in verses 7–12.

## The defeat of the dragon

'There was war in Heaven.' Michael the archangel ('arch' means 'chief'—there is only one archangel in the Bible) is fighting with the angels against the dragon and his angels. The dragon and his angels are not strong enough and they lose their place in heaven. The great dragon—that ancient serpent called the devil or Satan, who leads the whole world astray—is hurled down. He is cast out of heaven. Notice that the attack is Michael's and his angels'; they are the ones taking the initiative. 'Michael' means 'the one that is like God' which leads some people to think it is another name for the Lord Jesus Christ. I think not; but he is certainly the representative of the Lord Jesus Christ and he leads the attack. The initiative is always on the side of God; he is not 'backed into a corner' and finding himself having to do something against Satan. No, he takes the initiative, and the initiative is war in the heavenly, spiritual realms.

To what does this war refer? Since we know that Satan rebelled before the fall of Adam, this cannot be what is described here. This is not something that happened pre-creation or pre-Adam or pre-Fall. This is something that happens during and as a result of the ministry of our Lord Jesus Christ. We will see it referred to again when we come to Revelation 20, and the vexed question of the Millennium.

But here it is verses 9 and 10 that gives us the timing of this. 'The great dragon was hurled down—that ancient serpent called the devil, or Satan, who leads the whole world astray. He was hurled to the earth, and his angels with him. Then I heard a loud voice in heaven say: "Now have come the salvation and the power and the kingdom of our God, and the authority of his Christ. For the accuser of our brothers, who accuses them before our God day and night, has been hurled down."'

So the question is: when did our Lord Jesus Christ receive authority? There is only one answer; he received it as a result of his cross, resurrection and ascension. So Jesus appears to his disciples at the end of Matthew's gospel and says 'All authority has been given to me.' That giving of authority is the casting out of Satan that is being referred to here. Jesus had already referred to it, before it happened, in John's gospel. In chapter 16: 11 he tells us 'the prince of this world now stands condemned,' and the context makes it clear the he is looking forward to the cross and beyond that, to his return to his Father. Even more tellingly in chapter 12, he says 'Now the Prince of this world will be driven out...' (verse 31). The Lord Jesus looks at the cross and says, in effect, 'What I am going to accomplish there is the driving out of the Prince of this world, Satan himself.' John no doubt remembered that prophecy, and now, here in Revelation, he says 'Yes; and it happened. There was war in heaven, and Satan and his angels lost their place in heaven.'

There at Calvary, Christ defeated Satan in (as it were) hand-to-hand combat. It is a mistake to think of the cross *only* in terms of atoning for our sins and purchasing forgiveness. It was a great battle, with the result, the apostle Paul tells us, that Christ triumphed over Satan and his followers by the cross, (Colossians 2:15). In the words of Hebrews, Christ 'destroy[ed] him who holds the power of death, that is the devil' (2:14). While Satan's final destruction is still in the future, as a result of the cross it is beyond doubt. Now, until the time of that final destruction, Satan has been cast out of heaven and is no longer allowed in.

Let us explore this a little further. Do you remember those puzzling words at the beginning of the Book of Job, where we are told that the angels gathered before God, and Satan came too (1:6)? What is he doing there? Just this: he is an angel. Though at that point he is already a rebellious angel, he is still an angel and has, as it were, a right to be in heaven. In the New Testament, though, that has changed. He who is the accuser of the brethren can no longer go before God, stand face to face with God and say 'He is only worshipping you because it pays him,' as he said to God about Job (1:9,10 and 2:4,5). That can no longer happen; Satan is now cast out. As I understand it, that is because the victory of God is no longer a potential victory, but an accomplished victory. Before Calvary, there was no doubt that God would win the heavenly struggle, but he had not *actually* won. But at Calvary God in Christ won the final victory. The Lord Jesus Christ now has won the right to shut the gates of heaven to Satan and his angels and say 'No entry! You are not allowed in. There is no more place for you here.' As a result, Satan is confined, the text says, not to hell but to the earth.

After his 'hurling down' has been stated in verse 9 and repeated in verse 10, verse 12 tells us that the heavens rejoice because the glory of heaven is no longer polluted by even the occasional presence of this monster, Satan: 'Therefore rejoice, you heavens and you who dwell in them!' But the rejoicing of heaven is not yet shared by all the earth; on the contrary, earth is to suffer: 'But woe to the earth and the sea, because the devil has gone down to you! He is filled with fury, because he knows that his time is short' (12:12). This is why the church suffers as it does in the Book of Revelation. It is why we can expect things to grow worse in our own experience and expect things to grow worse in the world as we draw close to the time of the coming of our Lord Jesus Christ. As Satan realises that his time is short and getting shorter, his fury is stirred up. A dragon is always, in mythology, a figure of fear. A furious dragon is a horrific being to face, and this is the being that the church faces.

## The rage of the dragon
Let us now think about the rage of the dragon as it is set out for us in verses

thirteen to the end. Because he is cast out of heaven Satan is furious, and he turns his fury against the woman—that is, against the church. He has no access to heaven and he has no access to Christ; the male child has now been snatched up and is on the throne of God. So the dragon can not get near him. He turns his attention to the church, but even the church is protected. She is given two wings of a great eagle so that she might fly to the place prepared for her in the desert (verse 14). The picture comes from the Book of Exodus, where we are told that God bears his people up on eagles' wings (19:4). As she flees, Satan unleashes a torrent, a flood against her. That torrent would have reached her and drowned her, but the earth opens up and swallows this flood of water.

So, what is he to do next? Having been thwarted in his attack on the church as the church, we are told he turns his rage against her offspring. 'The dragon was enraged at the woman and went off to make war against the rest of her offspring'—against, that is, individual Christians. The woman represents the whole church collectively, but the offspring are individual members—you and me. In his fury, it is to us that the dragon turns his attention. He can no longer accuse us before the Father in heaven, but he turns his rage against us.

## The secret: how to defeat Satan

So—let us get to the secret I promised you at the beginning of the chapter. How do we defeat Satan? We know that he prowls around as a roaring lion, looking for someone to devour (1 Peter 5:8). Satan and his many, many angels are constantly seeking to trip us and destroy us. Can we defeat him—and if so, how?

The answer is there in verse 11: 'they overcame him by the blood of the Lamb, by the word of their testimony; they did not love their lives so much as to shrink from death.'

Firstly, Satan is always defeated by the blood of the Lamb. Satan's primary attack on us is always going to be over our sinfulness. We never reach perfection in this life, and sometimes our progress in holiness seems painfully slow. The devil no longer has access to heaven to accuse us there, but he has access to our consciences still. How easy he finds it to discourage us! For when it comes to the reality of our sinfulness, he does not need to lie.

He does not even need to exaggerate. He lists our sins before us, reminding us all of every recurring sin. Each of us has 'sins of personality'; they seem to be so much a part of us that we make precious little progress however hard we work to subdue them and mortify them. How we can call ourselves believers when we are still showing those weaknesses, he asks. The only way to defeat him is 'by the blood of the Lamb.' It is futile to deny our sins; they are obvious to him and to us. So we face him, looking him straight in the eyes (metaphorically speaking!) and we admit, 'Everything you say is true, and worse. But Christ has died. The blood of Jesus Christ, God's Son, cleanses me from all unrighteousness.' That is what it means to take the blood of the Lamb as our plea when Satan accuses us. 'If you want to take my sin up,' we say, 'You must take it up with him. But you have no access there any more.'

We never can gain a victory by denying our sin, but only by admitting it. We gain no victories by promising to be better in the future, but only by pointing to the one who has paid the perfect, infinite price. As a hymn of John Newton's reminds us: 'I may my fierce accuser face and tell him: Christ has died.'[1]

The second aspect is closely linked with the first. The 'word of their testimony' refers simply to the believer claiming that blood for his own. It means that we appropriate the blood personally in our dealings with Satan: 'God has saved *me*; in *my* life he has moved; he has called *me* to Christ, I am one of his children.' That is the word of our testimony.

But there is a third thing, so important if we are *always* to defeat Satan. 'They did not love their lives so much as to shrink from death.' If you want to know how to defeat Satan always, and never again to fail before him, then this is it: prefer death to sin. Then, there is nothing he can do against you.

We looked briefly at this in the last chapter, and our Lord Jesus Christ made reference to it in Luke 12:4–5. 'I tell you, my friends, do not be afraid of those who kill the body and after that can do no more.' We smile at that in our materialistic age. 'Kill the body! Can do no more! What else is there?!' And the Lord Jesus responds: 'But I will show you whom you should fear: Fear him who, after the killing of the body, has power to throw you into hell. Yes, I tell you, fear him.' It is put slightly differently in

Matthew 10:28: 'Do not be afraid of those who kill the body but cannot kill the soul. Rather, be afraid of the One who can destroy both soul and body in hell.' Our Lord Jesus says 'If you would prefer to die than to sin, you are safe.' That is what is here before us. The only thing Satan can do to the believer is kill him; and frankly—if we have the proper perspective—that does not matter!

Let me illustrate. A few years ago, two very effective ministries came to an end at about the same time, but in very different ways. One was Fouzi Ayoub, a missionary to Muslims who took great risks to reach them for Christ. He was tragically killed on one of his journeys when his car hit a tree. Let us imagine that the rage of Satan was responsible for that. (I do not know that it was—directly—though we can be sure that Satan was furious at such an effective work, breaking down the prison that is Islam.) Four people were in the car, and only Fouzi was killed: it is the rage of Satan. At around the same time, the ministry of another man—whom I will not name—came to an end in a different way. His immorality—and his insistence on continuing in it—disgraced the church, and still does. His ministry came to an abrupt end, his books were pulped by his publisher and so on. Would it not have been better—to be frank—if that man had died suddenly, some years earlier? If we were given the choice, would we not prefer to be Fouzi, today, than him?

Those who do not love their lives so much as to shrink from death are immune from Satan. There have been times, of course, when God's people have literally been faced with the choice: sin or we kill you! Given courage by their Lord, many chose to die, because death does not matter! It takes them into the presence of their Lord. So when they said to Polycarp almost two thousand years ago 'Curse God, or die!' he replied 'Eighty and six years have I served him, and he has done me no wrong. How then can I curse my king, who saved me?' He chose death, rather than sin.

Christians have that perspective and should always have that perspective; there are things worse than death. We speak of 'a fate worse than death' and that is what sin is. Christians are—or should be—those who would rather die, than sin.

Added years of life are not always a blessing. In the Old Testament, Hezekiah was told by God that he was going to die. He pleaded with God for life, and was granted fifteen extra years. But in those years, he so sinned that the whole of Jerusalem was destroyed. For us, too, there are worse things than death. Death is called in Scripture 'sleeping with our fathers'; I once heard a well-known preacher remark 'Brother, better for you to sleep with your fathers tonight, than to sleep with your secretary tomorrow.' For myself, I so much fear disgracing the Lord that it is a regular prayer: 'Lord, if there is in my future such sin that will cause you public disgrace, take me home to glory before it!' The philosophers have problems with such a prayer; they are not sure that even God can know what I would have done if I had still been alive. But I am sure he can—and pray the prayer.

So in verses 13–17 we see the victory of God. The church is taken to the desert, and again the imagery is taken from the Old Testament. For though the desert *is* a desert, yet God's Old Testament people were looked after so very well there. Manna was provided from heaven, Moses their leader spoke face to face with God, there were supernatural leadings of the cloud by day and the pillar of fire by night. Even their clothes did not wear out! Remembering these blessings, Revelation picks up that imagery of the desert and the protection of God, and promises similar protection for the church throughout all the gospel age, and for all those Christians who would rather die than sin.

As we close the chapter, notice how he drives that home: 'the dragon was enraged at the woman and went off to make war against the rest of her offspring.' Who are the offspring? '... those who obey God's commandments and hold to the testimony of Jesus.' There is of course a link between obedience to the commandments of God and the gospel of the Lord Jesus Christ. It is always a danger that those of us who grasp that we cannot save ourselves by keeping the commandments begin to think that keeping the commandments does not matter; but if ever we think like that we are wrong. We cannot save ourselves by keeping the commandments because they are already broken, and we are already condemned: the law condemns us. But God's Spirit comes to us and he gives us new life and begins to dwell within us. There is a new love in our hearts, a love towards God and his commands. And the Lord Jesus Christ says '"If you love me, you will obey what I command' (John 14:15). Because we love him, we obey him and show our love by our obedience. It is clear: if we do not obey him, we do not love him, whatever else may be true of us. Here John drives that point home and says in effect, 'Those against whom Satan rages, those who are protected by God and overcome the evil one, are those who obey God's commands and hold to the testimony—the gospel—of Jesus.' We have not abandoned God's law for the gospel; not at all. We love righteousness, and we live righteously; we make the commands of God our delight.

Brothers and sisters, Satan—the red dragon—rages against the world. He rages particularly against the church of the Lord Jesus Christ. But do not fear him! The blood of Jesus is on your side, the testimony is on your side. Learn to hate sin with such a vehemence that you would rather die than sin. Then Satan can do nothing against you; he cannot touch you.

**Notes**

**1** From the hymn 'Approach, my soul, the mercy seat'.

# Princes and prophets, paradise and punishment

Please read Revelation 13 and 14

Chapters thirteen and fourteen have been 'happy hunting-grounds' for all kinds of strange ideas and dogmatic interpretations; if you have read the chapters through, you will be able to see why. We will stay well away from all such fancies, and continue our practice of standing well back to get a better view of the whole. That way, we may not have all our curiosity satisfied but we will be protected from serious error and silly statements that are proved wrong within a few years.

Revelation 12 has shown us the rage of the red dragon, and we saw that the dragon is Satan, the opponent of God. We began to see that he pours out his rage on individual Christian people, knowing that 'the church as a whole' is protected and always beyond his reach. Perhaps a question came into your mind as we began to think about that. Satan is a spiritual being and we are physical beings. How can a spiritual being have any effect on us? How can he persecute Christian people?

These chapters—13 and 14—introduce us symbolically to Satan's two great instruments for persecuting believers, and they are two great beasts. One beast comes from the land, and the other from the sea. In verse 1 the dragon stands on the seashore from where he can call to both the land and the sea, and as he calls to the beasts, one of them rises up out of the sea (verse 1), and the second (verse 11) out of the earth. Let us begin by looking at each beast in turn.

## The beast from the sea

The first beast is truly fearsome, even gruesome. As he comes out of the sea, he is described just as we would see him: first the horns, then the heads (plural, you notice). There are ten horns and seven heads. Each horn (not each head, as we might expect) has a crown, and each head carries a blasphemous name. Then we see the body, and finally the feet. But we no have time to concentrate on these before John's attention is caught by the fierce mouth, and it is the mouth of a lion.

Among many strange things about this beast, perhaps the strangest is that one of its heads has had a fatal wound that has been healed. I remember as a child asking if it was possible to recover from a fatal injury: why did 'fatal' always mean death? Was it not possible, at least occasionally, that someone could be fatally injured and yet recover? Naturally, I received the right and sensible answer: 'No, because if someone recovers from an injury it was not fatal.' 'Fatal' is a word we can only use after the event, once death has occurred. But here is a beast that does have a fatal wound and yet recovers.

We are given a clue as to who this beast is, or what it means, in verse 1. Remember that the background of the Book of Revelation is the Old Testament, and particularly the Old Testament apocalyptic writings in the Book of Daniel. Daniel's vision (chapter 7) shows us not one beast, but four. One of them is like a lion, one is like a bear, one like a leopard and one like none of these, but having horns. John's vision takes these four images and conflates them into one terrifying beast: lion, bear, leopard and ten horns. We will see the reason for the conflation in a moment.

From our vantage point looking back at history, we can know who Daniel's beasts are. In apocalyptic literature, horns symbolise kingship—which is why each horn in John's vision carries a crown. The kingdoms Daniel sees are clearly the kingdoms (or empires) of the Medes and Persians, the Greeks and the Romans.[1] These four are political powers that were still in the future in Daniel's day; all but one of them (the Romans) have passed by John's day.

But John's vision, unlike Daniel's, is not concerned with *particular* political powers. No, his vision conflates all these beasts to show us that this beast represents political power itself. Such power comes in many manifestations; though different kingdoms and empires rise and fall, political power itself is a constant. There is always somebody, somewhere, wanting to govern us! And just as political power is a constant, so is political tyranny.

This brings us to the head that was fatally wounded. Commentators suggest that this may refer to the Roman Empire. After the death of Nero that Empire looked as if it were about to crumble—as if it had been fatally wounded. Instead of dying, however, it survived and revived its power. Nearer to our own day, the Reformers saw this wounded head as a warning: the Roman Catholic church had been fatally wounded by the preaching of the gospel but it would revive. They were certainly right in their prophecy, though (as we shall see) I think they had the wrong beast! (It is the second beast, the beast from the land, that is concerned with false religion.) It is simpler, and safer, to say that the vision is simply telling us that when one political tyranny dies, political tyranny itself revives in another form. The beast is destroyed many, many times; but he always returns before long.

This Beast is very popular (verses 4 and 8), as political power tends to be. Self-interest suggests that we fall in with whatever political power is on the ascendant. Men worshipped the dragon because he had given authority to the Beast, and the whole world is astonished and follows the Beast, and they worship the Beast and say 'Who is like the Beast? Who can make war against him?' (verse 4). Again and again mankind thinks its hope lies in a new politics, in a new revolution—but all that happens is that one tyranny gives way to another. Some people, without any political interest, seem to see this and argue that there is no point rebelling against the powers that be. They are too powerful. So these folks concentrate simply on keeping their heads down and making whatever progress they can for their own comfort: the 'system' is here to stay.

So in picture terms we are being reminded that 'the whole world is under the control of the evil one' (1 John 5:19), and that Satan exercises his power through political machinery. We noticed in the last chapter that the true church does not wield political power; it is a 'wilderness' church. Now we are being shown that political power does not—usually at least—support the gospel. Instead, again and again political power is marshalled against the gospel.

In my own country, the United Kingdom, although we have been a Protestant nation for four hundred years, we have had only one monarch who was clearly an evangelical believer. There are one or two others that we might want to give 'the benefit of the doubt' to, and say they were 'hopefully converted'; but we can be sure of the evangelical faith of only one. He was Edward VI, the son of Henry VIII, the boy king who reigned for only a few years before his sickly health took him away. When Elizabeth his half-sister was on the throne, she pointedly refused to use her power to further the cause of the gospel. Her search for a 'middle way', which shaped the Anglican church for centuries, was merely a political move and not a spiritual one. She heard some fine Puritan preachers, and they preached some of the most pointed sermons imaginable, warning of the judgement of God on her and her dynasty unless she used that power to aid the kingdom of God. But Elizabeth listened to the sermons, frowned at the sermons—and ignored the sermons. Political power rarely moves to aid the gospel, because the whole world is under the control of the evil one.

Every earthly empire therefore that rises will be destroyed, because God always destroys his enemies. The Christian is not to be a follower of political schemes and dogmas; he is always separate from them. That is not to say a believer cannot get involved in politics; more believers should! But the Christian is always involved at one step removed. He never sees the hope of the world in a political party or a political revolution. He should never believe that any political power or party is God's party. Christians have unwisely, from time to time, formed Christian political parties. But history shows that the parties do not stay Christian for very long. We should not be surprised, nor disappointed; Christians are not followers of political schemes and dogmas for they have a higher king.

This beast arises then, and he persecutes the saints. He is given a mouth to utter proud words and blasphemies and to exercise his authority for forty-two months. (Again, let me remind you that we have seen that forty-two months, or one thousand two hundred and sixty days, or three and a half years, all refer to the whole gospel period.) So persecution and blasphemy continue throughout the Christian period.

But though it is a long age, it is a limited age. One day that age will come to an end. God has set its limits, and at the end his Son will come again and persecution will be at an end. But until then, and throughout that period, the Beast is persecuting the saints.

There is a strange mimicking of the Messiah in this Beast. He is called the one who was, now is not and will be; he is given that title in chapters

17:8,11—parodying Christ himself. In this chapter he is given authority over every tribe, people language and nation—again, like Christ himself (see Matthew 28:18 and Revelation 5:9). He commands wide influence, and the power he has he uses against the people of God and causes them great suffering. What should our response be? We cannot destroy this beast; it simply calls for patient endurance (verse 10). We remember again, as Jesus teaches in Luke 12, that all the devil can do—even under the guise of this first beast—is kill us. For the believer, that is not a tragedy: to die is gain (Philippians 1:21).

## The beast from the land

Now we turn to the second beast, in verses 11–18. This beast comes from the land and does not look nearly so terrible, but that only serves to make him more dangerous. This beast too has horns, but they are not very threatening. They are the horns of a lamb, more buds than horns, cute and maybe a little comic. But do not be deceived; there is nothing comic about this beast.

Though he looks like a lamb, he speaks with the voice of the dragon. He is still a servant of Satan, and he is a servant of the first beast too, since he exercises the authority of the first beast on behalf of the dragon. He makes the earth and its inhabitants worship that first beast, whose fatal wound has been healed.

But who is this beast? Let me test your Bible knowledge for a moment. Who do you know, in the Bible, that looks like a sheep but isn't one? If you know the gospels at all, you will know immediately that the answer is: false prophets. Our Lord Jesus Christ warns us about them in Matthew's gospel: 'Watch out for false prophets. They come to you in sheep's clothing, but inwardly they are ferocious wolves' (Matthew 7:15).

This is the same basic picture: someone who appears on the outside like a lamb, but hides his real nature as a servant of the dragon. So this beast represents false religion, and in particular—since he looks like a lamb—false religion that claims to be Christian.

But this beast does not only represent false religion. He is subservient to the first beast, which represented the power of the state. Hence, this second beast represents particularly religion that is tied closely to the state power.

History demonstrates what this picture should have warned us of: an 'established' church is always a bad thing.

Inevitably, not every church has recognised this down the years; only a few have consistently argued for the separation of church and state. They have seen that in the New Testament (as distinct from the Old), it is not the job of the church to promote the state, nor is it the job of the state to promote the church: they are two different spheres. They have recognised that when the church is an arm of the State, or when the State enforces religion, there you have the beast.

I do not want to be misunderstood here. In England, we do have an Established Church—the Church of England. There are still many fine Christian people and Christian teachers within that Church, and I am not saying that they are servants of the beast. But I do believe, and believe firmly, that it is a bad thing to have a church established by law because there you always have, at the very least, the possibility of the second beast. Some argue that it is a good thing to have Christian influence in the State in this way, that it brings many benefits. (Though living in England at the moment, it would be hard to say what they are!) But let us not be misled by apparent benefits, even if there are many. Scripture warns us against such a coalition.

When I was at school, things were very different than they are now. In the Junior School particularly we would stand at the end of every day, lift our chairs onto the desks (which would probably be called child abuse these days!) and stand behind our desks while the class teacher said a little prayer and sent us home. It was not a church school and had no links with any church or denomination at all. But we would pray ('Lord keep us safe this night, secure from all our fears; may angels guard us while we sleep, 'til morning light appears. Amen'), and we were taught Bible stories. Many people who are my age and above have similar memories, and we often lament the fact that this has changed. Perhaps we are wrong to lament it! True, we were taught the Bible stories, but most of us were taught them by unbelievers, and taught them in such a way that we were encouraged to believe they did not actually matter and were not really true! That was the beast, not the Spirit, and it is a good thing that those days have gone. It is undoubtedly true that it is hard to reach a world where two generations have grown up not knowing any Bible stories at all. It is true that we have in this country generations who do not even know who Moses is (unless he has something to do with Charlton Heston—or, more recently, with a Disney film). But perhaps in the long run we will find it is easier to deal with ignorance than to undo the false impressions that earlier generations received.

At any rate, the early church did not expect the State to do its job and they did not campaign for increased religious education in schools. They recognised that the State would always be an enemy. It would be the beast. Perhaps we need to recognise that this is the way it is going to be, for the foreseeable future.

## An unholy trinity

We have here an unholy trinity: Satan, the beast and the false prophet. Satan varies his attack: sometimes the first beast persecutes the church and sometimes it is the second beast. Always, however, his purpose is the same: to undermine the kingdom of God and to bring worship to the dragon.

Notice that this second beast can even use miracles: verse 13 says 'He performed great and miraculous signs, even causing fire to come down from heaven to earth in full view of men.' False prophets on Mount Carmel (1 Kings 18) tried to bring down fire from heaven, but could not. This beast can! Beware, says the New Testament, of lying signs and wonders (see for example 2 Thessalonians 2:9). This beast has miraculous powers, and uses that power to deceive. It is not uncommon today to hear miracles claimed by the followers of various false teachers, miracles that are used to underline false gospels. Gullible Christians seem all too ready to be deceived.

Next, this beast demands conformity. He forces everyone—small and great, rich and poor, free and slave—to receive a mark on either his right hand or on his forehead (verse 16). No-one can buy or sell unless they have the mark and so there is great economic hardship for those who refuse.

Commentators tie this into first-century experience where, in order to ply your trade, you had to be member of a trade guild. The problem for Christians was that these trade guilds were usually dedicated to some pagan God, and therefore Christians felt they could not be involved. Not being members, they could not work. Not being able to work, they could neither buy nor sell. They were persecuted because they would not wear the mark of the beast.

Notice that every inhabitant of the earth is marked; either he has the beast's mark, or he has the seal of the Lamb (7:3, 14:1). We all belong to one or the other—the beast or the Lamb. This is, I am sure, the main point of this mark. We do not need to be caught up with the flights of fancy that we often see about the mark of the beast. 'It's credit cards,' says one. 'Every credit card has the number 666 secretly in its background somewhere!' Or, 'The day is going to come when credit cards will have been replaced by a mark on the head or hand which we will show to some super-camera-computer, and that will be the mark of the beast.' No, no; it will not. Let me tell you how you know that it will not: those that have the mark of the beast cannot be saved. If you have one single Christian who carries that credit card or has the mark on his hand or behind the retina of his eye or wherever it may be—one single Christian proves it is not the mark of the beast. John is simply telling us in a dramatic and pictorial way that everybody either worships the beast, or they worship the Lamb, the Lord Jesus Christ—and that, whichever one we belong to, it will show.

## 666

What about the beast's number—666? Do not worry if you have it in your telephone number; it does not mean you are the beast. In ancient languages, letters had numerical value; numbers were usually letters, as they are, for example, in Roman numerals. Consequently, there has been a great deal of fun during the last two thousand years, working out whose name adds up to 666. It is no surprise that one of the prime candidates was the emperor Nero. (Though it has been rather caustically pointed out though that his name only adds up to 666 if you spell his Roman name in Hebrew letters—and make a spelling mistake while you are doing it. Somehow, this interpretation does not fill me with confidence!) Others, believing that the first beast is the final Antichrist and the second beast the last great false prophet who will unite religion and world government, believe we are being given a clue here that will help us identify him when he arrives: his name will add up to 666.

But there are, I think, two other possible solutions that are better than either of these. Some have pointed out that the letters in the name of Jesus add up to 888, and the early Christians would have known that. So this is a way of showing how inferior this second beast is. His name does not add up to 888, nor even to 777; only to 666. Or, similar but my own preferred interpretation: because the number 7 is the number of perfection, 777 would be the number of the Trinity. Here we have an unholy trinity; but it is deficient in every way. In every way he falls short. Though he apes God, and apes the Messiah, he cannot truly be compared to either. He is just a man. John is telling us that whatever this beast pretends, he is never more than a man: 'calculate the number of the beast, for it is man's number,'—the number of a man. He is only a man practising deception.

## Avoiding deception

Plainly, since the beast counterfeits true religion, we need to know how to avoid being deceived. How do we recognise those who are practising deception? Only by knowing the truth. Undramatic as it is, we must be like Timothy who was commanded 'Do your best to present yourself to God as one approved, a workman who does not need to be ashamed and who *correctly handles the word of truth*' (2 Timothy 2:15). Or as it says in Psalm 1, 'Blessed is the man who does not walk in the counsel of the wicked or stand in the way of sinners or sit in the seat of mockers. But *his delight is in the law of the Lord*, and on his law he meditates day and night' (Psalm 1:1–2)

There is only one way to ensure that we do not serve this beast: know the truth. As the Lord Jesus prayed 'Sanctify them by the truth; your word is truth' (John 17:17).

This is important. We live in a very anti-intellectual age, and most people—even many Christians—are more impressed by contemporary claims of miraculous powers than they are by an ancient book. Reading is neglected and it seems that the Bible is just too big a book for 'ordinary people' to study. But if they do not—and if churches do not teach the word to their people and do everything they can to make sure that 'ordinary Christians' know the Scriptures—then our people will go the way of the beast. Discernment comes by knowing the truth, and we get to know the truth by knowing the Bible, which is the truth. In it we find Jesus, who is the truth, and we are guarded from all error. 'It calls for wisdom.' It calls for getting stuck in.

Previous generations seem to have been so much better at this. A study of Puritan history will show that some Puritan preachers regularly preached for two hours, with their congregations crying out for them to go on longer. Those congregations generally had many 'ignorant and unlearned' men and women in them; it seems to be a strange comment on compulsory public education that people today cannot cope with such meat! But perhaps if God anoints his preachers again as he has done in past and Puritan days, even today's congregations will be crying out for them to go on, to preach longer and deeper sermons. We yearn for those days.

## Paradise and punishment

Now, let us look at chapter 14, which speaks of heaven and judgement. With all this persecution going on, the two beasts serving the dragon and persecuting the church of God, what is going to happen? In answer, we see heaven, earth and the great harvest.

Verse 1–5 is heaven. Again (see 7:4) we see the 144,000, people of the Lamb who have his name and his Father's name written on their foreheads; not the mark of the beast, but the mark of the true Lamb. All the redeemed in eternity have the Father's name on them, and they sing a new song. It can be only sung by the redeemed, and it sounds like harpists playing their harps, and like the roar of rushing waters and a loud peal of thunder. Last time we saw the 144,000 (7:4) they were on earth; now they are in heaven. In spite of the worst efforts of the dragon and the beasts, not a single one of God's people has been lost.

These people, we are told (and our translation is not particularly helpful) are those who did not defile themselves with women. Literally, it is just: they are virgins, and it means 'spiritual virgins'. The Bible is not anti-sex; this simply describes spiritual purity. It is the purpose of the gospel, says Paul, (2 Corinthians 11.2) to present us as a pure virgin to Christ. John uses that imagery here; these are those that are pure. They were purchased from among men and they are the fruit of God's work and the Lamb's work. These are those who, rather than hold on to a lie, held on to the truth:

'No lie was found in their mouths.' They loved the gospel, not the lie of Satan and his beasts.

In verses 6–13 we see what is happening on the earth. There are three more angels. The first angel flies in mid-air having the eternal gospel to proclaim. This reminds us that all the time that these beasts are raging and the dragon is waging his warfare, the gospel is being proclaimed and mankind is being warned of judgement to come. The angel is crying out 'Fear God and give him glory because the hour of his judgement has come.' This is no longer the day when God winks at sin: 'In the past God overlooked such ignorance, but now he commands all people everywhere to repent' (Acts 17:30). The day when sin must be judged has come and so all the earth must be commanded to fear God and to worship God. That is what the gospel does.

The second angel proclaims the downfall of paganism: 'Fallen, fallen is Babylon the great.' This is not the ancient literal city of Babylon; that has long since fallen. By the time that Revelation was written, Babylon was little more than a village. But Babylon symbolises Rome and all the pagan systems of the world with their spiritual adulteries and unfaithfulness to God. It has made all the nations drink the maddening wine of her adulteries (verse 8) and she is destroyed by it.

Then in verse 9–13, we come to the most solemn part yet. The third angel warns about the horrors of hell: 'If anyone worships the beast and his image and receives his mark on the forehead or on the hand, he, too, will drink of the wine of God's fury' (9–10). The punishment of hell is symbolised as torment with burning sulphur.

To say it is 'symbolised by burning sulphur' is not to be 'going soft' on the reality; symbols are (obviously) less real than the things they symbolise. Hell is therefore worse than burning sulphur; this is a picture of something horrific beyond description. It is also something that never ends, where there is no end to their suffering: 'the smoke of their torment rises for ever and ever. There is no rest day or night for those who worship the beast and his image… This calls for patient endurance on the part of the saints.' The saints obey God's commandments and are faithful to Jesus, and the reality of hell is just one motive for that.

Hell, thank God, is not for all: 'Write, blessed are the dead who die in the

Lord from now on … they will rest from their labour, for their deeds will follow them' (verse 13).

Then, in the final section, the horrors increase. Let us follow it through. 'I looked and there before me was a white cloud, and seated on the cloud was one "like a son of man."' Plainly, this refers to our Lord Jesus. He has a crown of gold on his head and a sharp sickle in his hand. Then another angel comes out of the temple and calls in a loud voice to him who was sitting on the cloud, 'Take your sickle and reap, because the time to reap has come for the harvest of the earth is ripe.'

So the Lord Jesus is told by an angel (that presumably comes from the presence of the Father) that the hour has come. Notice just in passing that while on earth Jesus said 'No-one knows about that day or hour, not even the angels in heaven, nor the Son, but only the Father' (Matthew 24:36). Even in heaven, it seems that is still true; the human nature of our Lord Jesus Christ still does not know when that hour is. So an angel comes from the Father and says 'Now is the time. Your Father has sent me with the word: begin the harvest.' Two harvests are mentioned, emphasising no doubt the thoroughness of this last, great, harvest. Then we get what is, I think, the most horrifying picture of the judgement that pen has ever committed to paper.

There is a winepress, and into this winepress are thrown grapes— representing the wicked. Then, the press begins to do what presses do: it presses, it crushes, it squeezes until the juice is squeezed out and runs out.

But of course it is not wine that runs out from this winepress, because they are not grapes that are in it: it is blood (verse 20). A tremendous amount of blood flows out, forming a river that stretches for 180 miles (1,600 stadia). For those 180 miles it is as high as a horse's bridle—perhaps 4 feet deep? This is God's judgement.

As I have repeatedly emphasised, John's visions are parallel, not consecutive. Yet at the same time, each succeeding vision seems to inch us closer to that final end; this is the fourth of the seven visions. In previous visions we have been brought up to the brink of judgement; but in this one we are brought right to its reality. We see the judgement of God described in horrific terms. Why have we had to wait until the fourth vision to see this?

Perhaps we are not allowed to see this until the visions have described just how wicked wickedness is; God has held back this picture until we see the depth and the extent of the appalling rebellion against God. But now that we have seen so much of the wickedness of the world, and the persecution of the church by the world, when at last the veil is taken away and we see the winepress and the blood flowing out from it we can say, 'It is horrible. But it is no more than they deserve.'

Let us remember, that is what Christians believe about hell: it is no more than the sinner deserves. We know that God is just. Hell, however horrible, is never, ever worse than those in it deserve. It is not the overflowing vicious anger of a God who has finally lost his temper. It is the soberly calculated, just deserts of those who rebel against him and stay in rebellion against him, refusing all his offers of mercy. The preaching of the gospel warns them, woos them and calls them to him, but they prefer the pleasures of sin for a season. Nobody in hell gets more than she deserves; though everybody there gets more than she thinks she deserves. For the redeemed, Heaven is infinitely better than they deserve. It is not justice that takes a person to heaven, but mercy and grace. But hell is about justice, and the damned get what they deserve, while the redeemed get what Christ deserves. If we got what we deserved, the hottest place in hell and the deepest place in this river of blood would be ours. But grace has made a difference. Refusing that grace and saying no to that offer of mercy in Christ makes this hell all the more deserved.

This is fearsome. Revelation is a fascinating book, but it is never light-hearted. And there is nothing here to point to annihilation. The idea that the wicked will just cease to be is, sadly, becoming increasingly popular even among evangelicals. But it is not supported by the Bible. Annihilation would be good news for the lost, would it not? But it is not so. If it were so, we would not need to preach the gospel; it would not matter. We could get on with enjoying our God and let the unbeliever get on with his life knowing that one day they would simply go to peaceful sleep. But it is not like that; their destiny is awesomely horrible. When the time has come, the judgement begins, and we escape because we are marked with the blood of the Lamb. The grace of God pardons us our sin.

We have nothing to boast of, but we do have a great work to do while it is still day. How can we fritter away our time? How can we compromise? How can we play, with the two beasts and the dragon, flirting with the world? How can we do anything but labour on, spending and being spent for those who have not yet the Saviour known? There are two beasts stalking this world, and they answer to the voice of the red dragon. Only Christ can rescue our friends from the beasts, the dragon and the winepress of awesome judgement.

**Notes**

1 For a straightforward exposition of this position, see **Stuart Olyott,** *Dare to stand alone* (Welwyn: Evangelical Press, 1982).

# Armageddon

Please read Revelation 15 and 16

Ｗe live in a strange world. While I was preparing the original draft of this chapter, the news was reported about the arrest of one of the youngest ever people in this country for mugging: he was five years old. His accomplice was nine. The story particularly caught my attention because it happened in Mexborough, South Yorkshire—my home town. Mexborough is not the first place you would think of as a problem area. Yet police spoke of their frustration since both the five year old and the nine year old were too young to be charged; there was nothing they could do. All the Inspector could say to them was 'Imagine if it were your Grandma that had been attacked.'

However, another article on the front page of the same newspaper on the same day might suggest that this would have made very little difference. It reported the story of the father who had spanked his 12–year old son for robbing his grandmother of £400. The *father* was sentenced to six months in prison. Our society knows it is crumbling—it can see the danger signs. Yet it is systematically removing everything that might stop it crumbling, while at the same time throwing up its hands in horror and saying 'What's gone wrong?'

The world has gone wrong. God gave law to the world to restrain evil, and authorised punishment when that law is broken. If we remove the idea of moral absolutes (that some things are always wrong) as our society has done, and regard wrong-doing as a sickness to be treated rather than a wrong to be punished, we end up inevitably with disintegration. We end up, in fact, heading for Armageddon—a society, a world, that is at war with one itself because it is at war with God and just cannot stand.

We turn in this chapter to Revelation 15 and 16, but we must look elsewhere first if we are to understand what is happening.[1]

When Pharaoh in ancient Egypt (Exodus 1–14) rebelled against God and refused to let the people of God go, God sent a series of ten plagues on the land. These plagues were warnings to Pharaoh to repent. Eventually, however, after Pharaoh had hardened his heart again and again, the time came when he had hardened his heart once too often and God's final judgement fell on him. It fell in two stages: first, the firstborn of each family died in one night, the Passover night (chapter 12). Second, the finest of his army were destroyed in one flood, as God parted the Red Sea for his own people to cross and then brought the walls of water crashing down, drowning the army that followed (Exodus 14). God had said 'Enough' and final judgement fell on Pharaoh.

When Herod (Acts 12)—one of the great Herod dynasty that was so significant in the life story of the Lord Jesus Christ—boasted about his power and accepted divine worship, God had reached the limits of his patience with Herod. This was a step too far. Suddenly, in the midst of life, Herod is struck dead. God says 'Enough' and final judgement falls on him.

Seven chapters earlier in the book of Acts, when Ananias and Sapphira set out to lie to God, it seemed to be such a very small sin. They simply wanted a reputation for generosity that they did not deserve—surely it would hardly matter? Who would care—who would know—if they used deceit to get the respect of the church? God knew, and God cared. We do not know how often God had reproved them for their sin prior to this, or whether this was their first step outside the boundaries of righteousness. But we do know it was the last step: God said 'Enough' and final judgement fell on them. First Ananias and then Sapphira died and were carried out from the presence of the apostles. In each of these cases, it was God's final judgement.

But it was not the Last Judgement! The Last Judgement is reserved for the end of the age, the end of the world. All mankind together will be judged by God on that awesome day. But before that awesome day for all the world, there are many awesome days for individuals and groups within the world. Individuals, communities and perhaps even nations come to God's final judgement before the Last Judgement: they reach the point at which God says 'Enough' and destroys them. In short, Scripture teaches that God has many 'final judgements', but only one Last Judgement. That is the key to everything in chapters 15 and 16.

Let us review briefly where we have got to so far.

## Review

Throughout the history of the world from the time of Christ to the end of the world, the word of God is preached. The Spirit applies it and churches are established: they are lampstands in a dark world (chapters 2–3). Again and again, God's people are persecuted by the world and they suffer many trials and afflictions—chapters 4–7. As a result of that, again and again God visits his judgements on the persecuting world (chapters 8–11). But the earthly conflict is no less than the outworking of the basic, fundamental spiritual warfare between Christ and Satan, the conflict between the seed of the woman and the dragon. Chapter 12 paints in broad strokes the reality of the conflict, chapter 13 shows us two of Satan's primary means of attack (political and religious persecution) and chapter 14 assures us of the safety of the redeemed and the doom of the lost.

Now in chapters 15 and 16, we are introduced to seven final plagues. They are final in the sense I have tried to illustrate above; with them, God's wrath is completed (15:1). These are the plagues that show that God's patience is at an end. The plagues sound like God's last judgement; and they are—but they are not! They are merely 'final judgements' for those who go too far. Each and every one of them foreshadows in some way the great Last Judgement to come.

So we see seven bowls being unveiled, the bowls of God's wrath. These bowls refer to the same things as the seven trumpets, back in chapters 8–11. There we saw seven great warnings from God, judgements that fell as warnings to the sinful people to repent. They were trumpet calls of repentance.

But of course, for some they were more than warnings. For some, they were fatal. A third of the people died and were ushered out of this life. For them, they were the final judgements, the final plagues that took them to eternal judgement. While the rest of the world is still being warned, their warning period is at an end. Chapters 15 and 16, then, turn to the way those judgements affect those who are removed, those for whom they are the end.

What we are being told is that God acts throughout history, and he acts in judgement. There are thousands of judgements and a wide variety of ways that God judges, and it is those judgements that these chapters are about. Let us turn then to the chapters.

## Heaven

Chapter 15 shows us heaven. Usually, in these parallel visions in Revelation, we *end* in heaven. But this one is different. This time we start there. In heaven, we are told, there are those who have been victorious over the beast. The beast is the servant of Satan, and in heaven—gathered by the glass sea before the throne (verse 2—compare with chapter 4)—those who have been victorious hold harps and sing. Heaven is full of praise; they are singing the song of Moses and of the Lamb.

The song of Moses is the song recorded in Exodus 15. When the Red Sea closed around the pursuing Egyptians, Moses sang 'I will sing to the LORD, for he is highly exalted. The horse and its rider he has hurled into the sea' (Exodus 15:1). It is a magnificent song of God's judgement and mercy. But in heaven they are also singing the song of the Lamb, and that song is given to us: 'Great and marvellous are your deeds, Lord God Almighty. Just and true are your ways, King of the ages. Who will not fear you, O Lord, and bring glory to your name? For you alone are holy. All nations will come and worship before you, for your righteous acts have been revealed' (Revelation 15:3–4). Notice that when dreadful judgements are about to fall on the earth, those in heaven—who really know God and are themselves free from sin—say 'Just and true are your ways, O Lord.' Here on earth, those of us that know God also know that his ways are just and true. Sometimes, though, unbelief still has a part of our hearts and pulls us back into doubt: how can such awful judgements be righteous and merciful? But once we are in the glory, once we are gathered by that sea of glass and see things as they really are, even the most awesome and awful judgements will produce no complaint from us. The judgements of God merely serve to emphasise his holiness: if God had not judged the way he has, he would not be righteous. Holiness demands the judgement of sin.

## The open temple

Then we get the vision of the temple open in heaven. The temple is open because the great veil, which once barred access to the Holy of Holies, has been removed by our Lord Jesus Christ, (Matthew 27:51). Out of the temple come seven angels with seven plagues. One of the four living creatures around the throne gives the angels these bowls. The angels come out from the temple in order to emphasise that the judgements that are about to be described come from the presence of God. They are not accidents. When catastrophes happen in the world, they are not interruptions to God's government of the world, events that he did not plan and cannot quite cope with. Rather, they are part of his sovereign government of the world; they are things that God himself has sent. We will not spend too much time on these plagues, but let us at least glance at them.

The first plague is recorded in 16:2. Ugly and painful sores broke out on those who wore the mark of the beast and bore his image. Several of these plagues do bear a striking resemblance to the plagues of Egypt, and this is one. That battle in Exodus between God and Pharaoh was one manifestation of the ongoing battle between God and Satan, so it is not surprising that these plagues should be picked up and applied here. There are some people for whom the last call to repentance is this kind of dreadful sore; the things that usher them to judgement and hell are sores and ulcers. God's people are exempt from this plague.

But of course, you may say, God's people may suffer ulcers and sores and boils. Yes; but in their case they are not the plagues of judgement. For them, they work for good, not evil (Romans 8:28).

The second plague turns the sea into blood, like the blood of a dead man: thick, cold, drying and stinking. For many of course it is the sea that ushers them to judgement. The Hebrews hated the sea; for them, when people came from the sea, they were almost always enemies. They hated it. It was a place of terror for them. It is appropriate therefore that John picks this up as a judgement of God.

The third plague is the rivers turning to blood. Rivers are generally calmer than the sea, but they too are dangerous and may take life. When it happens, notice again that there is no reproach to God. The angel in charge proclaims God's holiness, and that the punishment of those who perish is just: 'They have shed the blood of your saints and prophets, and you have given them blood to drink as they deserve' (16:6). They wanted blood, and they have got blood. It is a dreadful thing: God often gives people exactly what they wanted, but he gives it them as punishment. Those under the altar, the saints themselves who have been slain, also admit that God is just: 'Yes, Lord God Almighty, true and just are your judgements.'

The fourth plague involves the Sun. The bowl is poured out on the Sun and the Sun is given power to scorch with fire so that people are seared by the intense heat. They curse the name of God. God's people are given a promise in Psalm 121 that the Sun will not hurt them; but for some people, the Sun is a devastating judgement. Not enough Sun and the crops cannot grow; too much Sun and the same crops are scorched. Here, the *people* are scorched, not just the crops. Yet these people—we note with awe—curse the name of the God who has control over these plagues, refusing to repent and glorify him. That is very true to life, is it not? When we turn to the philosophers and ask them if there is a God, they will reply, often, in terms of the problem of evil. 'Look at the things that happen in the world,' they say. They do not call them judgements; they call them tragedies or disasters—and such they are. But they do not say to themselves, 'Yes; these things fit well with what the Bible says God is like. The Bible warns us that God hates sin, and that the wrath of God is being revealed from heaven against all ungodliness and unrighteousness. These disasters, therefore, are evidence of the existence of the God of the Bible.' Instead, they say 'How can there be a God of love when there is so much suffering?' Or they say defiantly 'If there is such a God, I don't want to worship him if he allows these things.' And so they blaspheme the God who has power over the plagues. Like a prisoner promised release on repentance but who continues to defy the authority of the courts, so these men and women seal their own destruction.

The fifth plague is poured out on the beast himself. Anti-Christian government plunges people into darkness. 'His kingdom was plunged into darkness.' We saw in an earlier chapter that this beast represents godless government and it is salutary to see how the Western world—which has done so much to reject God—now finds itself floundering in ever increasing darkness. It does not know what to do. When its citizens cry out for relief, all the beast can do is extinguish even more of the light! (Hence, the point of the story at the beginning of this chapter.) Our children are attacking elderly people, and yet Britain has it easy! In the US, children of five and six and seven are taking guns to school and shooting their peers. In 1955, a survey in the United States asked high school children to list the things that worried them most about school. The things that they listed included:

people talking in class; not getting their homework done; spit-balls in their hair. The same survey was done in 1995, with the same questions asked. The answers this time were: drugs in playground; guns in the school; teenage (and younger!) pregnancies. In a mere 40 years, it has become a completely different world! Yet it often seems that all the governments can do—in the name of enlightenment—is go further and further down the same road that has produced this chaos. It is the judgement of God as the kingdom of the beast is plunged into darkness.

For this reason, if for no other, older people need to have patience with the young. Our young people today are facing things that we never faced at their age. One survey recently suggested that in some areas of Britain half of *ten-year olds* are sexually active! We need to understand the world our own young people live in and we need to be encouraging young Christian warriors fighting on a battlefield they are hardly prepared for.

The sixth plague leads us to Armageddon itself, and the very word needs some explanation. Revelation 16:16 is the only place in the Bible where the word 'Armageddon' is used. Do be careful of those who build too much on this! When the Jehovah's Witnesses come to your door, they will want to talk to you about Armageddon. The reason is simple: they do their door-to-door work in order to earn enough 'brownie points' for them to escape Armageddon themselves. Naturally then when they knock on our doors the subject has a tendency to obsess them! But this is the only place where it is mentioned.

Armageddon is the place of the last battle, and the name comes from an Old Testament story. In Judges chapters 4–5, Barak—under orders from Deborah—wages war on the apparently invincible Canaanites, and God himself comes to their aid as Barak wages war and defeats those Canaanites. The place of the battle is Megiddo, from which we get the word Har-Magedon, or Armageddon. Hence, it becomes a symbol of every time when the people of God are about to be destroyed and God comes to their aid. That, says John here, is what will happen one final time. The water of the river Euphrates dries up, making an easy road from Babylon. Babylon—as we will see again—is a potent symbol of everything that is anti-Christian. So the waters of the river Euphrates are dried up to make a way for the enemies of God to gather together for battle. Though there are many times when God has suddenly intervened to rescue his people, this passage does seem to point to one last conflict, one last battle, one last time when the forces of Satan try to destroy the church of Jesus. God's people, oppressed and distressed beyond endurance, cry out for deliverance, and Christ himself appears to their rescue.

Remember, this is a symbolic book: it does not follow therefore that we are to expect demons to become incarnate and rank up alongside the river to fight the angels on the other side alongside the people of God. Instead, the symbolism portrays vividly the one last time when the forces of evil are unleashed on the church. This time it is so powerful, it is so amazing, that it looks as if the church herself is going to be destroyed. Then, the Lord himself descends from heaven with a shout, in blazing fire destroying his enemies (2 Thessalonians 2). These evil spirits that look like frogs, spewing from the mouths of the dragon, beast and false prophet, emphasise the evil of the encounter. The final conflict will have Satan behind it, and anti-Christian government and anti-Christian religion as its weapons. Then, the Lord gives instructions for his people to take care: 'I come like a thief. Blessed is he who stays awake and keeps his clothes with him' (verse 15). Christian people, when this battle is raging do not go to sleep!

But we must not panic, either. The command to keep our clothes with us is also symbolic. Clothes symbolise righteousness often in Scripture, and so Scripture is exhorting us here not to turn away from our righteousness under pressure. And since our true righteousness before God is only the righteousness of Christ reckoned to our account by faith, we are being exhorted not to abandon our faith in the face of enormous suffering. Instead, we are to stand by the God we have trusted in. Wait for him; he is coming. He will come like a thief, and we must be ready. 'Keep yourself in God's love' is how Jude puts it (Jude 21). It must be a priority!

Pastors time and again have to counsel Christian people who have slipped far from God, and have to say 'It really is up to you whether you walk with God or not. You *can* walk away; you *can* go to sleep. But you *must not* walk away; you *must not* go to sleep.' Salvation in Christ is not simply a matter of a once-for-all decision, with the rest of life being easy. It is a walk. We must walk with God, and stand by our standards. We will deal with this more a little later, and think more of how we are to 'keep our clothes with us.'

Here then is this dreadful warning. The Scripture has a great deal to say about the triumph of the gospel, and I believe we have yet better days to come in terms of the world-wide growth of the church. But at the same time, Scripture says there are hard days coming, and there is a last battle.

Now the seventh bowl appears without delay; the end is near. So we are told in verse 17 that it is finished at last; it is done. Judgement begins: the great city of Babylon splits into three parts. The nations collapse. God has not forgotten Babylon's sins, and he gives her to drink the wine of the fury of his wrath. The very land is destroyed as punishments fall from heaven and the end is here. (More of this in the next chapter.) We know that the time will come when the Lord Jesus himself will descend from heaven with a shout. He will punish with blazing fire all his enemies. His enemies will continue *until* that very day; the church can expect no rest until then. But his enemies will not continue *beyond* that day. An earthquake is mentioned here and none like it has been known since man has been on the earth. It surely is the earthquake that is referred to in Hebrews 12:26–13:5:

'At that time his voice shook the earth, but now he has promised, "Once more I will shake not only the earth but also the heavens." The words "once more" indicate the removing of what can be shaken—that is, created things—so that what cannot be shaken may remain. Therefore, since we are receiving a kingdom that cannot be shaken, let us be thankful, and so worship God acceptably with reverence and awe, for our "God is a consuming fire." Keep on loving each other as brothers. Do not forget to entertain strangers, for by so doing some people have entertained angels without knowing it. Remember those in prison as if you were their fellow prisoners, and those who are ill-treated as if you yourselves were suffering. Marriage should be honoured by all, and the marriage bed kept pure, for God will judge the adulterer and all the sexually immoral. Keep your lives free from the love of money and be content with what you have, because God has said, "Never will I leave you; never will I forsake you."'

## Basic godliness

Since such a time of rage of the red dragon is coming, and a last battle is coming and there is one more time when the church is going to be crushed under persecutions—how are we to live? 'Stay awake and keep your clothes with you,' is the instruction we are given. But what does that mean?

Specifically, it means that we are to pay attention to those things mentioned in Hebrews 12:26–13:5. We are to worship: to carry on worshipping God with reverence and awe. We do not forget who God is, nor cease to serve him—it is basic. 'Worship' in the New Testament extends to the whole of our life, as Romans 12:1 makes clear: 'I urge you, brothers, in view of God's mercy, to offer your bodies as living sacrifices, holy and pleasing to God—*this is your spiritual act of worship.*'

Then, Hebrews instructs us to continue in brotherly love—the Christian life is a communal thing, not a private thing. So we are to serve one another in the grace of hospitality. We must care for the unfortunate and visit those who are in prison. In context, this refers to the godly who are in prison for their faith. They are not to be abandoned just because they are now suffering; we must not think of them as an embarrassment in any way. We must not think they are not worth bothering with: they are God's chosen ones. Then, says the apostle, watch out for your family life and sexual purity—do not give in on this, even though every part of the world tells you to give in. Finally, keep yourselves free from the love of money.

All this sounds rather basic. Could not God say something more startling? Could he not give us some vast task to do before the earthquake comes and rips apart our society? No; that is the point. Godliness *is* basic. It is not about the things that so often seem to excite the church: shivers down the spine, transports of delight, rolling around roaring like wild beasts, casting out demons or handling snakes. That is not godliness: basic godliness is about honouring God in our lives and defeating Satan and the beast by refusing to sin even if it costs us our lives.

To put it another way, as times grow worse, the church needs to take increasing care to preserve her purity. It is not a matter of turning inwards, which is always a danger. It is always easy to adopt new programs and new ways for strengthening one another and yet forget that this is only a means to an end. To turn inwards is fatal. But we do need to make sure that we have firm foundations in every area of our lives.

Things are getting worse! Perhaps it's a sign that I'm now middle aged; maybe the middle aged always think things have got worse.

When I were a lad, the times they were bad,
But not nearly as bad as when me dad were a lad.
When me dad were a lad, they were almost as bad
As when me dad's dad were a lad!

(Source unknown)

Perhaps. But objectively, surely, what is happening in our society is a sign that things are getting worse. Things that were completely unacceptable only two decades ago are now applauded by society at large, and it's getting worse. The attempted removal of the notorious 'Clause 28' is one example of this. About half of those serving jail sentences for paedophilia would not have committed an offence at all if the age of homosexual consent were sixteen. Just as homosexuality gradually became acceptable (as someone put it, 'from the love that dare not speak its name to the love that cannot keep its mouth shut in less than one generation'), so it seems now that the same pressure groups are moving towards legalising what we still call child abuse. Yes, even while our society throws up its hands in horror at the very idea of child abuse, parts of that society are quietly working to legalise it. It is not just in sexual matters that standards are slipping; that is true. But this is the most obvious way in which society is coming to pieces.

Are we at the very end time? I do not know; but this I am sure of: times of ease for the church are at an end. What then must we do? We must reform ourselves and become true puritans. That is, we must become a people concerned with the purity of life and doctrine. We must examine our personal lives, our family lives, our church lives, our work lives and our national lives by the Scriptures. We must apply ourselves in every realm to reform.

In our personal lives, we have to stop pretending about godliness, and get down to prayer and the study of the word. We must stop flirting with the world—it is always dangerous, but now it is fatal. In our families, we have to concentrate on building godly family units. The world will not help us in this; when we send our children to school, attempts will be made to dismantle systematically the values we endeavour to instil in them. Churches have to work at ways of helping parents to be distinctively

Christian parents. We have to encourage reform in our church lives, examining the word of God to see what is essential and what is not—and then to stop falling out about things that are neither here nor there. (I have lost count of the number of articles I have read suggesting that those who use the NIV are—knowingly or otherwise—the servants of Satan. The world rushes to hell while the people of God squabble about which imperfect translation is the best translation! How these things must break the heart of God!)

We have to be prepared to take our stand for Christ and integrity at work knowing that it will hurt and might even cost us our jobs. We have to send some of our best thinkers and people into society to change society. We need genuine Christians to stand for parliament, and then (before and after election) to stand openly for what is right, to stand up on the hustings and say 'This is wrong, that is right. That is what I am going to stand for'—and if they lose their seats, they pay the price. In no other way will we recapture the minds of the people.

Spurgeon said about the Puritans 'There were giants in the land in those days, and we are all pygmies today.' He was probably right, but it is a disconcerting thought. For the Puritans lost all their major battles, and we who are smaller and weaker must win ours.

Armageddon—the war against God—is going on around us at this very moment. The beast is among us. To wear his mark is to perish, but to have the seal of God on our foreheads, that is glory.

**Note**

1  I am particularly indebted at this point to Stuart Olyott both for the distinction between 'final judgements' and 'the last judgement', and for the illustrations given to make the point.

# The fall of Babylon

Please read Revelation 17 and 18

L et me begin this chapter by quoting a prayer. It is a strange prayer in some ways, for it was a public prayer but it has bite. Rev. Joe Wright was asked to open the new session of the Kansas senate in prayer. In itself, this causes some of us some surprise; after all, in the United States the separation of church and state is taken so seriously that a pupil cannot carry his Bible into school. Nevertheless, the custom persists, it is a good custom, and this is the prayer Joe Wright prayed:

'Heavenly Father, we come before you today to ask Your forgiveness and to seek Your direction and guidance. We know Your Word says, "Woe on those who call evil good," but that's exactly what we have done. We have lost our spiritual equilibrium and reversed our values. We confess that:

- We have ridiculed the absolute truth of Your Word and called it pluralism.

- We have worshipped other gods and called it multiculturalism.

- We have endorsed perversion and called it an alternative lifestyle.

- We have exploited the poor and called it the lottery.

- We have neglected the needy and called it self-preservation.

- We have rewarded laziness and called it welfare.

- We have killed our unborn children and called it a choice.

- We have shot abortionists and called it justifiable.

- We have neglected to discipline our children and called it building self-esteem.

- We have abused power and called it political savvy.

- We have coveted our neighbour's possessions and called it ambition.

- We have polluted the air with profanity and pornography and called it freedom of expression.

- We have ridiculed the time-honoured values of our forefathers and called it enlightenment.

Search us, O God, and know our hearts today; cleanse us from every sin and set us free. Guide and bless these men and women who have been sent to direct us to the centre of Your will. I ask it in the name of Your Son, the living Saviour, Christ. Amen.'

As he was praying, a number of legislators walked out in protest. But in six short weeks after that, the church where Joe Wright is pastor logged more than 5,000 phone calls, with only 47 of them negative.

Perhaps, though, we can understand why some of the legislators walked out. In these days, it is a remarkable—and to some a dreadful—thing when the ministers of God begin to behave as if they *are* the ministers of God! The Old Testament prophets spoke God's judgement on the sins of the nation, but woe to the minister today who, in public, points his finger at the sins of his own nation and culture! It is very easy to condemn and ridicule and weep over the sins of another culture and ignore our own, but every culture has its sins and every nation has its favourite sins.

## Two cities
The book of Revelation could be said to be about two nations or two cities, growing together side by side. One is the city of Jerusalem, the heavenly Jerusalem, and the other is the city of Babylon. They are allegorical cities, symbolic of the two ways of living and the two choices every man, woman and child has.

We have seen repeatedly that there is radical hatred between Satan and his servants (the city of Babylon) on the one hand, and God and his servants on the other hand. We have seen that the world, under the control of Satan, persecutes the church of Jesus Christ. We have noticed that when religious power is tied to the State, all too easily the two together become agents of Satan; the church of the Lord Jesus Christ is not necessarily to be identified with the church that calls itself by that name. The professing church of Jesus may in fact be apostate and have gone over to the other side. When it does, the true church is persecuted by the false church, and this has happened repeatedly in the world.

We come now to the last but one section in the book. We have worked our way through five of the seven parallel sections of the book, sections that deal with the same period in history. We have said that the period referred to is the whole gospel age, that time from the ascension of our Lord Jesus to his return in glory. We have noticed that as we progress through the book each section takes us a little closer to the reality of judgement. As we have progressed the pace has increased, the imagery has become more vivid and compact, and there is a sense of approaching climax. We now come to the fall of Babylon.

Babylon has been mentioned by name before, and chapters 17–19 focus on it and speak of its downfall. It is not the literal city of Babylon on the banks of the Euphrates that is being spoken of; that city had already fallen. At the time when John writes, it is little more than a ruined village. Rather, it is the fall of what that city represented.

## Babylon viewed (17:1–6)

This part of the vision opens with a woman, a prostitute, sitting on a scarlet beast. The scarlet beast is covered with blasphemous names, and it has seven heads and ten horns. Though we have not met the woman before, we recognise this beast. We have met two beasts, and one of them did have seven heads and ten horns, though we were not told his colour. But we were told the colour of his master: the beast served Satan and Satan was a red dragon. Here, it seems that the beast and his master have combined into a composite image. That should not surprise us, because as we get closer to the end of the book the imagery becomes more compact to indicate the nearness of the coming climax. The dragon and the two beasts were all enemies of God, and we were told how they would be defeated. Now though we see only one beast—all the enemies of God are represented in one rather horrible symbol. It is even a crude symbol: a prostitute, sitting on a beast. What does the symbol mean?

Mankind, says the Bible, is not an accident; we were created for a purpose. We were created to be in intimate union with God and, in particular, in intimate union with the Lord Jesus Christ. Our proper role is to be the bride of Christ; it is a common picture in Scripture.

Another picture describes us as the New Jerusalem. Jerusalem was the city where God dwelt. In the city was the temple and in the temple was the Holy of Holies, and inside the Holy of Holies was the ark of the covenant. Above the ark was a light, the shekinah glory, the symbol of the presence of God on earth. This was the place where God was. Mankind is meant to be the place where God lives; the temple was meant, pictorially, to represent human beings—the place where God dwells. That is why, when we come into the New Testament era and the temple in Jerusalem is destroyed, it is the church (1 Corinthians 3:16) and individual Christians (1 Corinthians 6:19) that are described as God's temple.

Back to the picture of the bride. Even marital or sexual love is meant to reflect the relationship between Christ and the church. To say this does not denigrate the relationship between Christ and the church; instead, it elevates marital love to its proper place and helps us, perhaps, to understand why sexual sin is so serious. This is how we were meant to be. It is God's purpose.

This prostitute though represents mankind as he is. We are not in intimate union with God. We are God's bride, but we are living in a parody of the intimacy we were made for. A parody, after all, is all that a prostitute can ever offer. We live in a parody of divine intimacy with anything and everything else: with the world, the flesh and the devil, or with commerce, politics and religion. With anything! But it is not a loving relationship. We may give ourselves to these things, but it is a mercenary and ugly thing, not a loving and beautiful thing. It does not have the radiant, lasting beauty of a true marriage but the cheap ugliness of a relationship with a prostitute. We should be the heavenly Jerusalem, but we have become a spiritual Babylon. Thus, the whore and Babylon are one and the same; they picture our failure to be what we should be and show us that we are, by nature, perversions of what we ought to be. Babylon and the whore therefore both represent man in rebellion against God. The whore rides the scarlet beast: she is carried along by the devil himself. There is no suggestion that the beast has reins and stirrups, so that the whore can control it. She does not so much ride the beast as sit upon it, carried away by this bucking bronco of Satanic influence.

False religion—and even no religion is false religion: if you do not worship the one true God you serve something, even if only yourself—is always represented in Scripture as spiritual adultery. It is mankind being unfaithful to his maker. In Ezekiel 23, it is referred to as prostitution: 'When she carried on her prostitution openly and exposed her nakedness, I turned away from her in disgust, just as I had turned away from her sister. Yet she became more and more promiscuous as she recalled the days of her youth, when she was a prostitute in Egypt. There she lusted after her lovers, whose genitals were like those of donkeys and whose emission was like that of horses. So you longed for the lewdness of your youth, when in Egypt your bosom was caressed and your young breasts fondled' (verse 18–21). It is rather shocking imagery; speaking like this, I suspect Ezekiel would not be invited back to many pulpits. To criticise a nation's sins would be bad enough, but is he not going too far with his crude imagery? But this is the word of God and God uses its shocking language to express how he feels about those who live their lives without him. They are spiritual harlots and they are in a filthy relationship with the world, the flesh and the devil.

Harlotry is always filthy, whatever its appearance might be. Notice that this harlot in chapter 17 carries an illusion of greatness. She is dressed in purple and scarlet, and carries a golden cup in her hand. She is an impressive looking lady—but the inside of the cup reveals the truth. It is filled with abominable things: it is filled with the filth of her adulteries. She is a drunken harlot and drunk not with alcohol but with the blood of the saints (verse 6). Ever since Cain, the world has persecuted and murdered the saints of God. She is the mother of prostitutes and of all the abominations of the earth.

## Babylon interpreted

What then does Babylon mean? John sees the marvels of this woman: the purple and scarlet dress, the glittering gold and valuable pearls. When he sees her he is 'astonished'. The word used in the original indicates a degree of admiration—it is the same word used in 13:3 of the world admiring and wondering at the beast. It seems that John, this mighty servant of God who was so close to the Lord Jesus Christ—even John who endures persecution for his faith in Jesus—for a moment is dazzled by the allure of world. There is something grand about this woman, though she is filthy. John is still in the flesh. He is still human. We can certainly understand him, for we too know what it is to be dazzled by the world and its glories. We may sing:

Fading is the worldling's pleasure,
All its boasted pomp and show.

Or:

I'd rather have Jesus than silver or gold …

It is true, and we mean it when we sing it. But it does not mean that we never find the world attractive. It does not mean that we never find this whore attractive and our hearts running after her. Like John, we are still human. We understand John so well!

The angel, however, does not understand him at all. The angel is flabbergasted at John's response, and says in effect, 'Why are you astonished? What on earth is impressing you? Can you not see past the clothes and the golden cup? Can you not see what is inside? Let me show you what is really happening: I will explain to you the mystery of the woman and the beast she rides.'

So the angel explains: the beast comes from hell itself, and will return to it. The beast, like the whore, may impress the world for a while. In particular, his seeming invulnerability is impressive: he was, now is not, and will come again. (This is a phrase similar to ones we have met before, in 1:4 and 13:3, where it was used about Christ and God respectively. But he is not to be compared with the King, who once was dead and is now alive, and alive for evermore. Jesus was and is and is to come; there is no genuine comparison between the two.)

'Let the world admire the world,' the angel seems to say. 'Let the world admire the beast and its rider: you, believer, ought to know better. You should know what is really going on, and keep your mind elsewhere.'

Then, the angel uses a phrase which suggests that the following words will be difficult to understand. 'This,' he says, 'calls for a mind with wisdom' (verse 9). Many commentators are very specific about the meaning of the following verses, but differ widely from one another. These commentators identify at least tentatively the five kings or kingdoms (the word could mean either) and the one who is and is to come. The beast who was and now is not is an eighth king (11), and they identify him too. Then they turn to try and identify the ten horns who are ten kings who have not yet received a kingdom but will do so for a short time, receiving authority along with the beast. Various interpreters link these with Roman emperors, and it is possible to do that. Barnett,[1] for example, sees the five who have fallen as Augustus, Tiberius, Gaius, Claudius and Nero. The one who is, is Vespasian, the one who is still to come and will remain a little while is Titus. Then the eighth king is associated with Domitian. In John's day, it was widely believed that brutal Nero would return from the dead and resume his place as emperor and Barnett argues that Domitian is seen by John as a kind of 'Nero-reincarnate' (hence, he belongs to the seven) who is destined for destruction. Barnett then identifies the ten horns who are given authority to reign for an hour as governors in senatorial provinces who only govern for a year.

For all kinds of reasons however, it is difficult to identify any of these people with any certainty. We will content ourselves with noting the important thrust of the message: all the kingdoms of the world are under the control of the evil one. They only endure for a time. They receive authority (verse 12) but it is the authority of the beast. With that authority they always make war against the Lamb. Sadly, this is always true: even when a nation arises that has godly government for a while, it never lasts very long before the power of government is again turned against the Lamb and his followers.

But the Lamb will overcome them in the end (14) because he is the Lord of Lords and the King of Kings. With him will be his called, chosen and faithful followers. Notice how it is put. It does not say 'The Lamb, with his called, chosen and faithful followers, will overcome them.' The reason for this is that the Lamb does not need our help to overcome. We are the battleground (as it were) but he does not need our support for his victory.

## The city and the chosen

In John's day, the evil he is speaking about is undoubtedly represented by Rome—hence the reference to the city on seven hills ('the seven heads are seven hills on which the woman sits' verse 9) because Rome, as is well known, is built on seven hills. But that Roman Empire which set out to crush the Christian church and instead crumbled around it is just one manifestation of the ongoing war between the world and the church, between Satan and the Lamb.

Let us think for a while about those people that the Lord of Lords and King of Kings has with him: they are described as 'called, chosen and faithful'. These are very powerful descriptions of the true Christian.

Christians are a *called* people. They are people whom the gospel has reached, and who have been regenerated (born again) by the Holy Spirit. They have not just heard the gospel; by the grace of God they have responded to it. Jesus said 'Many are called ('invited' in the NIV) but are few are chosen' (Matthew 22:14); but that is not what is meant by 'called' in this verse. That is what is called the 'general call': when the gospel is proclaimed and explained and Jesus offered to those who hear it. A general call, or invitation, even a command is issued to all who hear the gospel: repent and believe. But there is, too, in the Bible another way the word 'called' is used. The call referred to here in Revelation is that calling spoken of in the great 'golden chain' of Romans 8:30: 'Those he called he also justified.' There are some people who, when the gospel is proclaimed, have it driven into their hearts by the Spirit of God. A good picture of conversion is that of Jesus at the tomb of Lazarus. Lazarus is dead and his body is already rotting; he has been dead for four days. But when Jesus says 'Lazarus, come out,' life goes somehow with the words of Jesus, the flesh of Lazarus is restored, and his spirit re-enters his body. The inevitable result is that Lazarus comes out. Similarly, when the gospel is proclaimed, there are people that God calls in that life-giving way. Without that special call, no-one would ever respond: 'The man without the Spirit does not accept the things that come from the Spirit of God for they are foolishness to him, and he cannot understand them' (1 Corinthians 2:14). Without the work of the Spirit, the gospel ('the things that come from the Spirit of God') cannot be understood and received. As the Lord Jesus said, 'I tell you the truth, no-one can see the kingdom of God unless he is born again' (John 3:3). It is God the Spirit who sovereignly chooses where he works: 'The wind blows wherever it pleases. You hear its sound but you cannot tell where it comes from or where it is going,' says Jesus (John 3:8), 'so it is with everyone born of the Spirit.' When the Spirit works ('Spirit' and 'wind' are the same word in Greek) you cannot see him any more than you see the wind. You can only tell where he has been by the effect he has. The Spirit of God calls some of those who hear the gospel in a powerful, effective way: they are given spiritual life, and they respond. Why does he call some, but not all, in this way? Because they are chosen.

Christians are a *chosen* people. Back in Revelation 17, verse 8 makes reference to those whose names have *not* been written in the Book of Life from the creation of the world. It is another way of saying they are not chosen; they are those who remain unconverted. Chapter 13:8 speaks of the Book of Life belonging to the Lamb slain from the foundation of the world and all those whose names are not there are the ones who worship the beast.

The doctrine of God's election, or choosing, which the apostle is teaching here is obviously a great mystery. It is, though, a mystery that is clearly revealed in the Bible. Out of the vast mass of sinful humanity—corrupt, putrefied humanity, rotten and sinful humanity—God, in infinite grace, has chosen certain specific individuals. He has written their names in the Lamb's Book of Life, and he wrote them there before the creation of the world. Even before the creation of the world, God in amazing grace was determined to save them. He gives his Son to be their Saviour. In the plan of God, the Lamb was slain before the creation of the world (13:8) for them. In time, God ensures that the gospel comes to them and that, by his Spirit, they respond: they receive faith as a gift (Ephesians 2:8). They are saved because they are called and they are called because they are chosen.

How do we recognise them? It is not that they spend all their time talking about being chosen. It is not that they study with great zeal the decrees of God so that they can talk in learned tones about 'infralapsarian' and 'supralapsarian'. We recognise them because they are faithful followers of the Lord Jesus Christ.

Christians are a *faithful* people. We recognise them because they have faith. They *believe* the faith and they *keep* the faith. They do not fall away, they do not change sides, they do not go over to the enemy. They remain faithful.

Now perhaps someone is reading these words who is not converted and is now wondering: 'If these things are true, how can I know whether God has chosen me before the creation of the world?' There is one infallible way to know, but only one. It is not by examining your forehead to see whether the number of the beast is there. It is not wishing you could pry into heaven and find the secret decrees of God—the Lamb's Book of Life—and look for your name. There is one infallible way to know that God chose you before the creation of the world, and it is this: repent of your sins, and believe the gospel. Then you will know, without a shadow of doubt, that God chose you in eternity. It is the only way of knowing—before the end of the age. You are not to look at yourself, to see if you have certain qualifications. You are to look at Christ, who died for sinners, and trust him. For those who will come with the Lamb are his called, chosen and faithful followers.

Let us move on. 'The angel said to me 'The waters you saw, where the prostitute sits, are peoples, multitudes, nations and languages' (17:15). This demonstrates again that it is not the literal city of Babylon; peoples, multitudes, nations and languages are represented as being her seat. Then we are told in verse 16 'The beast and the ten horns you saw will hate the prostitute. They will bring her to ruin and leave her naked; they will eat her flesh and burn her with fire.' Some see this as a future split in the ranks of evil, and perhaps there will be such a split. But more than that, surely, we are being told that Satan hates the world, even when he dominates it. We must never imagine that God and Satan both care for us, like two suitors for a woman's hand, with each believing she will be happier with him. It is not that Satan and God both care, and both want us to enjoy ourselves, but simply have radically different ideas of what that would mean. God says 'Blessed are those who keep my law' and Satan says in effect 'Blessed are those who eat, drink and make merry, and break free of the law of God.' But Satan is a liar; he does not offer the delights of the world out of love, but in order to destroy. He offers these things so that, at the right time, he can turn on those he has deceived and devour them. He may strip you naked and leave you in the streets for everyone to see; burned with fire, consumed and destroyed (verse 16). Satan hates mankind. He hates the people of God, certainly. But he hates his own people as well. He is full of hate, and delights to destroy. Only the Lamb is able to redeem and to save. The Lamb is not a liar, nor the father of lies, and when he said 'I have come that they may have life and have it to the full' (John 10:10) he knew what he was talking about and was sincere in his desire.

This is an important message to learn. The media gives us a different message, forever suggesting that godliness is restrictive, narrow and boring. So often, government seems to give the same message too. But we must remember that even when there are fine men and women in the media or the government, the institutions themselves are controlled by the beast. Education will also tell us a different story, and insist that Biblical ideas are outdated now. Once more, even from the towers of learning, it is the beast who speaks. We can even find *churches* that will tell us to ignore the Bible and the gospel and the absolute standards they both demand—but that is the beast, too. The beast will destroy. He will open eyes to the pleasures of sin but never show they are 'for a short time' only (Hebrews 11:25). He will insist that it is fun to revel in the paths of unrighteousness and then, when men have followed him, he will turn on them and rip their hearts out. It is the way the beast operates.

How is this evil ever going to come to an end? That is what we are shown next.

## Babylon's fall, judgement and disappearance

Babylon's fall is announced in chapter 18, and announced in the past tense because it is that certain. 'Fallen, fallen is Babylon the great' (verse 2), 'She has become a home for demons and a haunt for every evil spirit, a haunt for every unclean and detestable bird.' As I have said, by the time Revelation was written, the real city of Babylon had become a destroyed wreck of a city. Living in its ruins would be all kinds of unclean and detestable animals. That foreshadows what will happen to the evil kingdoms; the whole world system will mirror her fate when the Lamb finally says 'Enough is enough.'

The picture we are given is of a city that is not only ruined but infested: infested with demons and evil spirits and every kind of detestable bird. Because her destruction is already so certain the cry goes up 'come out of her my people so that you will not share in her sins.' Through the preaching of the gospel, represented here as the call to come out, those whom God has chosen are (in old fashioned language) savingly awakened. They are asleep in their sins, and then God's voice sounds in their ears and they wake up. They are dead in their sins, and the voice of Jesus comes to them and says, 'Live.' They are called out of this city: they leave its values behind.

A strange idea, that people can be saved and continue to live a worldly and sinful life, has become popular recently. It is the beast! No-one can have Jesus as Saviour and not have him as Lord, and it is only ever the beast who insists otherwise. Those who do not 'come out of her' will share in her sins and will receive her plagues: 'Come out of her, my people, *so that* you will not share in her sins, so that you will not receive any of her plagues' (verse 4).

The rest of the chapter is taken up in amplifying the dreadful destruction. God has said 'The city is going to be destroyed.' She is going to be paid back for her sins, and he calls out. He calls out to those of us that are Christians, and he says 'do not compromise with this system.' Here is the city, here is the world. She might look grand, but she is a whore. Come out: have nothing to do with her. Then, so that we may have the force of this call impressed upon us, the rest of chapter amplifies how dreadful her destruction will be.

This destruction comes suddenly, we are told in verse 8. The same thing is then repeated in verses 10 and 18 and 19, emphasising the shock of the world at her destruction. Who would have thought it? We Christians are in a minority: we cannot win a single battle. Children at school are now being given a telephone number to use if their fathers smack them! How can we win in that situation? Only today I have read a forecast by a renowned Christian commentator that Islam will be successful in its attempts to destroy Christendom. It is easy to see where he gets such an idea! We can only triumph because the Lamb will fight for us, and when he does the destruction of the world and its systems will be a shock to the world. She will not be expecting it. Destruction will come like a thief in the night, like labour pains on a pregnant woman. How can God's kingdom triumph? It will triumph because it is God's kingdom, and God will pay back Babylon. Verse 6 says that God pays her back double for what she has done.

However, 'double' does not mean, here, 'twice as much as she deserves.' That would be unjust, and God is never unjust. It is more like the meaning of the word when we say that one man is another man's double. It means there is an exact correspondence between their features. Here, it means there is an exact correspondence between Babylon's sins and Babylon's punishment. It has the same meaning in Isaiah 40:2, when we are told God's own people have received double for their iniquity.

The most appalling thing about the world and its destruction is that she will receive precisely what she deserves: like for like. It is a fearful thought.

Because evil is represented as a city, her woes are represented as things that would portray a city in trouble. Hence, merchants weep and sea-captains see her destruction far off, and so on. We do not need to go into details with the rest of the chapter.

'Come out of her my people.' This is the world; this is the world system. This is the evil city of Babylon in which we live. This is the great whore that rides the beast. This is the enemy of God that is going to be destroyed. And God says to us, 'Come out. Don't compromise.' Each of us must examine our own lives. What does God want us to do from now on to show that we have heard his call to 'come out of her'? Which of the world's values have we adopted? What lifestyle or habit needs to be repented of and left? Left, that is, because it reinforces Babylon's values in our own heart, and woos us away from the Christ who redeemed us, and whom we serve with joy and gladness?

## Note

1 **Paul Barnett,** *Apocalypse now and then* (Sydney: Aquila Press, 1989).

# A tale of two suppers

Please read Revelation 19

Some of you may remember the continental holidays that were very popular in the late sixties. You know the type, advertised as 'six countries in seven days', in some quarters they got the nickname 'If it's Tuesday it must be Belgium'. You may perhaps have begun to feel a little like that about the Book of Revelation; we have been moving rather fast. Moving fast is deliberate! We are trying to get an overview of the main message rather than focus on interpreting every detail. But if your head is spinning, you might be glad to know that in this chapter we will look at only one of Revelation's chapters. It is an awesome chapter though, and well deserves the attention.

Chapter 19 records the second half of the sixth vision, the sixth, remember, in a series of seven parallel visions. As we have seen, although the visions are parallel there is also a sense of progression, with each vision taking us nearer to the very end. This chapter reveals horrific descriptions of the last judgement; it is important to have read and understood the earlier chapters, or we will not appreciate that this horrific judgement is also a just judgement. Without Revelation's descriptions of the horrific nature of wickedness—the 'exceeding sinfulness of sin' (see Romans 7:13, AV)—its descriptions of judgement will certainly seem 'over the top'. One of the many problems of our age is that sin has become something of a joke. Indeed, it is hard to find anyone who takes it seriously—unless, perhaps, it is a terrorist outrage or the abuse of children. But one great message of the Bible is that *God* takes sin seriously, always. It is a sad sign of the extent to which the church has taken on board the values of the world that even some sections of evangelicalism no longer believe in hell. A proper meditation on the gruesome pictures of chapter 19 might help restore a proper sense of solemnity to Christian people.

We have already seen that this section describes again the long war against God, and describes evil, or mankind in sin, by means of two pictures: a whore, and the city of Babylon. Picturing evil as a city emphasises that evil is organised, and picturing it as a whore shows the impurity of life without God—that the world is not what it was meant to be. Mankind is not in the bridal relationship with the Son of God that we were created for, but has become instead no more than a harlot who prostitutes herself for every passing lover.

As we enter this chapter the long war against God is coming to a close, and we are introduced to two suppers. The first is the wedding supper of the lamb, and the second is the great supper of God. Though each one is described as a supper, they are two very different events. By the end of the chapter, the war is over—and it is very clear who has won. The two suppers indicate the victory.

## The wedding supper of the Lamb

The first supper then is the wedding supper of the lamb, described like that in verse 9:

'Blessed are those who are invited to the wedding supper of the Lamb.' The earlier verses show us the bride having made herself ready for this great banquet, wearing fine linen, bright and clean. Like the previous visions, then, this one too ends in heaven, and we get a glimpse of it. But what a glimpse it is this time! There is a roar of a great multitude shouting 'Hallelujah! Salvation and glory and power belong to our God.' Twenty-four elders respond to a description of the torments of hell by shouting 'Amen, Hallelujah,' and a great multitude sounding like the roar of rushing waters and the rumble of great thunder cry out 'Hallelujah! For our Lord God Almighty reigns.'

This of course is the passage that Handel based his famous 'Hallelujah Chorus' on, and he did us a great service when he set this to music for us. Very few, though, who solemnly stand when this point in 'The Messiah' is reached realise that these songs celebrate the righteous act of God in condemning the lost to hell!

The day of judgement has finally arrived, and we are at a wedding party. Everything at last is ready for the greatest party of them all; it is the wedding party of the Lamb, and the bride has made herself ready (verse

7)—though we do not see her yet. This is the reality that Jesus spoke of in the parable of the banquet (Matthew 22:2–13).

The Lamb and the bridegroom is of course the Lord Jesus Christ. Revelation has shown us many pictures of him already; we saw him in chapter 4 for example, sitting on the throne of God. Now we have arrived at the moment that all eternity has been waiting for. Indeed, it is no exaggeration to say that this is the moment the whole universe was created for. This is the moment when the Lord Jesus Christ receives his bride, the moment when the Father gives the nations to his Son as a bridal prize.

Psalm 2 speaks of this moment, and gives us a tiny glimpse into heaven before the world began, a glimpse into what theologians have called 'The Counsel of Eternity.' There the Father offers the Son a great prize: 'Ask of me, and I will make the nations your inheritance, the ends of the earth your possession.' It is a time when there is no time, a time when there is only Father, Son and Holy Spirit. In effect, the Father says to the Son 'You can see down the corridors of time yet to be. You can see what will happen. If you ask me, I will give you an inheritance, the very ends of the earth. I will give you a people for yourself.' This is what Jesus refers to in John 17:6 : 'They were yours; you gave them to me.' This moment, before history even began, is still the decisive moment in history. If the Son asks for that prize, then he will have to pay for the gift his Father will give him. If he asks for a bride, he will have to purchase that bride with his own blood. Of course, the Son asked, and human history took its course. Knowing what it would mean for him, the Son gladly asked for and accepted the bride his Father offered. Here at last in Revelation that bride—those people—are being presented to him. The marriage of the Lamb has come.

So, the great multitude in heaven sing the praise of God, the praise—that is—of Jehovah ('Jah' is an abbreviated form of Jehovah, and 'Hallelujah' means 'Praise Jehovah). At last, the inhabitants of heaven can, as it were, relax; the victory is accomplished. It was never in doubt, for God is supreme in power and might; but now, at last, it is done. 'Salvation and glory and power belong to our God, for true and just are his judgements. He has condemned the great prostitute who corrupted the earth by her adulteries.'

Evil is ended, and heaven rejoices at the smoke of the torments of the damned. 'Hallelujah, the smoke goes up from her for ever and ever' (verse 3).

Whose torment is it, precisely? The harlot's, that great prostitute who corrupted the earth by her adulteries (verse 2). At last, ungodliness has been judged and judged righteously. God is too good to have acted out of malice or vindictiveness: 'true and just are his judgements.'

There is a positive side, too, to the rejoicing of heaven. They rejoice at the coming marriage of the Lamb, and sing as the bride of Christ is presented to her great bridegroom without spot, blemish or any such thing, 'Hallelujah; for our Lord God Almighty reigns; let us rejoice and be glad and give him glory! For the wedding of the Lamb has come, and his bride has made herself ready' (verse 6).

But how has she made herself ready? The answer is that she is wearing 'fine linen, bright and clean,' and 'the fine linen stands for the righteous acts of the saints.' Only the truly righteous can be fit to be a bride of the King of righteousness! But is this not a problem? We are all sinners; our most righteous acts are polluted. How then can we explain the bride wearing garments without any spot or blemish? Though you probably know the answer to this very well, we will return to it later. It is crucial to our whole understanding of the purpose of God.

Then, the angel underlines the certainty of this revelation by telling him 'These are the true words of God' (verse 9). John misunderstands that. He thinks, for a moment, that the angel is telling him that he—the angel—is God himself. Inevitably, then, John falls to worship the angel, but he is rebuked. Throughout the Bible, whenever anyone righteous is offered worship, they rebuke the worshippers: Paul and Barnabas, for example, do that in the Acts of the Apostles (Acts 14:14–15). It is all the more worthy of note, then, that when the Lord Jesus is offered worship by Thomas (John 20:28), far from rebuking Thomas, Jesus accepts the worship. It is his due; he is God the Son. But this angel is not the Lord Jesus. He is just a fellow servant with John—a ministering angel given to those who are heirs of salvation (Hebrews 1:14), or 'a fellow servant with you and your brothers and those who hold to the testimony of Jesus' (verse 10).

## Fine linen, righteous acts

Now, let us turn back to those righteous acts, and ask where the bride got them. To answer, we must turn our eyes away from the bride. Here comes the groom; the trumpets have sounded and the King has been announced. Suddenly (verse 11) he is here: 'I saw heaven standing open and there before me was a white horse, whose rider is called Faithful and True. With justice he judges and makes war. His eyes are like blazing fire, and on his head are many crowns. He has a name written on him that no one knows but he himself. He is dressed in a robe dipped in blood' (11–13).

We saw a rider on a white horse once before (6:2) and we noticed then that there are different opinions as to his identity. But we are left in no doubt who *this* rider is; 'his name is the Word of God' says verse 13, and that of course is one of John's favourite titles for Jesus. When he appears, he is not alone; the armies of heaven are following him. They too are riding on white horses and they too dressed in fine linen, white and clean. Comparing verse 8 with verse 14 shows us clearly that this army of heaven is another picture of the bride.

But there is a great contrast between the rider at the head and the soldiers that follow. He, this great king at the head of the procession, is not dressed in fine, clean linen. He is filthy with blood. It is not simply that he has been splashed with blood; the literal reading of verse 13 tells us that his robe has been 'baptised' or dipped in blood. Every part of his robe is bloody.

Pause a while to let the glory of this sink in. We, the bride of Christ, are clean. But we are clean only because he is filthy. Because he has stained his robes, our robes are fine linen, bright and clean. The robes we wear have been *given* us to wear (verse 8). They are not ours by nature or because we have earned them. They have been presented to us by a groom who himself has to wear a robe dipped in blood.

Like the whole book of Revelation, it is a picture, of course. It is a picture of a great and fundamental doctrine—the doctrine of imputation, or the great exchange. By nature, we are all sinners. Sin is so much a part of us that even our righteous acts are as filthy rags, says the prophet (Isaiah 64:6). But even that is a very polite, very British translation of what Isaiah says. More literally, Isaiah says the very best acts we ever can do are like a filthy menstrual cloth. It is a deliberately offensive picture because we are not, by nature, a pretty sight! In fact, our sin causes us to be offensive in the sight of a holy God. But then our Lord Jesus Christ comes into the world. He is not like us. He comes without sin. His robes are *not* filthy rags. They are spotless and seamless, white and bright. But then, having lived a spotless life with no thought or word or deed ever polluting that life, he comes to the cross to die. His death is the wages of sin; death always is (Romans 6:23). But he has no sin, so how can this be? Ah, says the Bible, he pays on the cross not for his own sin, because he has none, but for ours. Our sin is taken by God and reckoned (imputed or credited) to the account of the Lord Jesus Christ, and his righteousness is reckoned to our account. In picture language, he takes my filthy robes and he wears them himself, and he takes his righteous robes and he clothes me in them. That is what John is picturing here.

Paul puts the same truth for us in propositional terms; where John uses words to paint us a picture, Paul uses them in a more formal manner. This is how he puts it: 'But now a righteousness from God, apart from law, has been made known, to which the Law and the Prophets testify. This righteousness from God comes through faith in Jesus Christ to all who believe. There is no difference, for all have sinned and fall short of the glory of God, and are justified freely by his grace through the redemption that came by Christ Jesus' (Romans 3:21–24).

A righteousness from God has been made available, says Paul. Martin Luther, the great German reformer, testified of the freedom that finally understanding this truth brought him. For a long time he read it as 'the righteousness *of* God' and thought it was a righteousness that God demanded. No matter how hard he tried, Luther knew he could not match the righteous demands of God. But when he finally realised that it meant, instead, God's own righteousness that he *provides* freely to those who trust Christ, his soul was set free and the world was never the same again.

Yes, says John, that is what I'm talking about. It is a great exchange; the Lord Christ takes our filthy rags and he gives us his righteous robes. We are set free. We are made ready to be the bride of Christ. Then at the end of the age, when the Lord Jesus Christ descends in glory, it will be obvious to all that the one who is coming as conquering King is also the Saviour who died. It will be obvious to all that those who are with him—whether we speak of a bride or of armies—are white and bright and righteous. They are perfectly righteous because they have the righteousness of Jesus. And the righteousness of Jesus is the righteousness of God, the righteousness *from* God that is for all who believe.

Then this King begins his rule. As his word, the sword of the Spirit, has won the allegiance of millions, so now he rules the rest with a rod of iron— verse 15 quotes Psalm 2. He has another sword that strikes down the nations, a sharp sword. The victory over Babylon and evil is his victory alone; he is the true King. There are many crowns on his head, for he has won many victories. He is the great battle leader, the King of Kings and the Lord of Lords. This is the great marriage supper of the Lamb.

## The other supper

But there is a second supper in this chapter. Verse 15 tells us that the Lord Jesus 'treads the winepress of the fury of the wrath of God Almighty.' What does that mean? We saw the winepress in 14:19–20 and it is a horrible and sobering picture of the torments of the lost: 'The angel swung his sickle on the earth, gathered its grapes and threw them into the great winepress of God's wrath. They were trampled in the winepress outside the city, and blood flowed out of the press, rising as high as the horses' bridles for a distance of 1600 stadia (about 180 miles).' This is a river of blood some four feet high and 180 miles long; it is a frankly revolting picture of the wicked being trodden like wine in a press. Here in chapter 19 we are told who is doing the treading down, who it is who is torturing the lost. Look at this carefully, and only speak with reverence: for it is Jesus: '*he* treads the winepress of the fury of the wrath of God Almighty'—he and no other.

Is he then a monster, this Jesus of ours? No—away with the idea! He is the Lamb of God. This one who goes on to tread the winepress of the fury of the wrath of God is the one who first lay down his life for sinners. He is the one who said to sinners 'Come to me, all you who are weary and burdened, and I will give you rest' (Matthew 11:28). He is the one who deliberately, knowing what he was doing and what it would cost him, left heaven's glory in order to be a redeemer for sinners. He is the one who sent his Spirit into the world and who all down the centuries has been pleading with men and women to turn from their sin and to come to him. He is no monster—he is the Prince of Peace! This winepress is a tragedy that ought never to be; but the time comes when God the Father, God the Son and God the Spirit say to those who reject him 'Enough! No more!' We noticed in an earlier chapter (Chapter 6) the reference to the wrath of the Lamb (6:16) and commented that it is, in some senses, a ridiculous picture. An angry Lamb! But it is not ridiculous when the Lamb is Jesus—it is awesome. If Jesus the loving Saviour, the sacrificial Lamb of God, can be made angry, then how great the offence must be. If the loving God of heaven must punish sin in a way that is fitly described in this picture, then how appalling sin must be. It often does not seem that appalling to us—but how would we know? We were born in sin. It is our natural habitat. We no more know the filth of sin than a rat notices the foul smell in the sewers.

I can only think of one thing worse than the torments of hell. It is this: the knowledge that those torments are inflicted by the Prince of Love. What would it be like for you to endure under his wrath day after day, eternity after eternity, always and for ever knowing that once, if you had only asked him, he would have saved you? Can you imagine the horror of that?

## Complete triumph

Then in verse 19 and following we are shown that his triumph is now complete. Though his enemies are gathered to make war, there is no war. They are simply destroyed. Ever since time began, a long war against God has been waged. Revelation tells us that it continues to the very end, and grows in ferocity immediately before the end. It may even look as if the church may be about to die. The armies of Satan gather and the enemy is strong. Just before the end there is one, final, enemy—as Paul puts it (probably referring to the same events) the lawless one will be revealed whom the Lord Jesus will overthrow with the breath of his mouth and destroy by the splendour of his coming, (2 Thessalonians 2:8).

This lawless one has won obedience, says 2 Thessalonians 2, by false miracles; the false prophet here (verse 20) has false miracles. Here then is a gathering for a last battle as the enemies of God are confident of victory. But to their surprise, there is no battle to be fought! Jesus comes and the gates of heaven are thrown open wide. The groom—the Lamb—rides out on his white horse, and the splendour of his coming destroys his enemies, finishing them off for ever and ever. The beasts—the first beast and the false prophet who is the second beast—they are thrown into hell, the fiery lake of burning sulphur (verse 20), the place prepared for the devil and his angels. Thus begins the second supper, the great supper of God.

I hardly know how to write about these verses; let me quote them. It may be enough! 'Come, gather together for the great supper of God, so that you may eat the flesh of kings, generals, and mighty men, of horses and their riders, and the flesh of all people, free and slave, small and great' (verses 17–18). In response, in verse 21, after the two beasts are thrown into the lake, the rest of them—the kings of the earth and their armies, the enemies of the Lamb, are killed with the sword that came out of the mouth of the rider on the horse, and all the birds gorge themselves on their flesh.

Can I put it like this? The destiny of every one of us is a supper; either the great supper of God or the marriage supper of the Lamb. But those who find themselves at the great supper of God are not guests. They are the meat course. It is not a jest; there is nothing remotely funny here.

Why does the Scripture use such barbaric imagery? Surely it can only be for this reason: so that the ungodly will take their coming punishment seriously. It is as if God comes to them again and again and again, with every serious picture that omnipotence can produce. 'There is fire that burns without ever stopping. That causes you no fear? Then let me speak of everlasting darkness, and a place of weeping and wailing and gnashing of teeth. Do these images reach you, and stir you from ungodly complacency? No? Then let me try another: let me speak of a place where the birds come and gorge themselves for all eternity on your flesh. Will nothing get through to you?' That is what God is saying to us; let us understand the image, and take his loving warning seriously.

Some professing Christians like to speak of the Bible's teaching of hell like this: 'Biblical imagery of hell is just that,' they say. 'It is an image, a picture, not the reality.' True, but the picture of a fire is not as hot as the fire. The pictures of hell are not as awful—or as awe-ful—as the reality. God wants the ungodly to take their coming punishment seriously, to flee from the wrath to come. Men and women joke about hell; how easy it is to dismiss something if only we can make a joke of it. So they say things like 'heaven for the climate, hell for the company.' Is this the company they want? Birds that gorge on their flesh? For if so, hell is most certainly the place to go!

Let all who read this ensure that they are part of the marriage supper of the Lamb. The angel said, and John wrote, blessed are those who are invited to the marriage supper of the Lamb, (verse 9). How do you make sure you are part of it? You come as a sinner to Jesus, and you say 'Lord, have mercy on me.'

Is it that simple? Yes, it is. Do you know the story of Naaman the leper (2 Kings 5)? He heard that there was a prophet in Israel, Elisha, who could cure him, so he prepared for the long journey and went to see Elisha. When Elisha heard of his arrival, he merely sent him a message: 'Go and bathe yourself in the river Jordan, and you will be clean.' The leper was both affronted and annoyed: 'There are rivers in my own land, far better than the Jordan,' he said So he went away with the leprosy still on him.

But his servants, who respected him and cared for him, said 'Master, if he had asked you to do something hard, would you not have done it? Why then do you rebel at this?' So Naaman went and washed himself in the Jordan and the leprosy left him.

It is included in the Bible as a picture of our cleansing from the leprosy of sin. Many people are not even aware of their sin, but some of those who are become affronted by the simplicity of salvation. They are told that they must come as a sinner to Jesus, and say 'Lord, have mercy on me a sinner.' There is nothing else to do, nothing else to say. They would rather make an effort! They would rather be given some great task, some great law to keep. But while ever they let their affront keep them away, they are lost. But if they come, as sinners, to Jesus, he will save them. He will change them. He will take them to the wedding supper of the Lamb, and make sure that they are never at the great supper of God.

# The Millennium

Please read Revelation 20

Finally we have arrived at the last thrilling section of the book of Revelation. We must divide it into two parts, looking at chapter 20 now, and chapters 21 and 22 in our next chapter.

Revelation 20 is the most argued-over chapter in the whole book, with great and godly men taking very different views. Yet the more I read this chapter and consider each phrase, the more convinced I am that its meaning is very clear and the chapter is not difficult to understand. It speaks of a thousand years—a millennium—and it is the millennium that is at the heart of the controversy. There are at least four main views about the millennium, and before we look at the chapter itself we do need at least to mention each of these views. It needs to be said that each of these views had in the past, and still has in the present, able and godly defenders.

## Pre-millennial

First, there is the pre-millennial view: the return of the Lord Jesus Christ is before ('pre') the millennium, and in fact it ushers in the millennium. Pre-millennialists hold that after the return of the Lord Jesus he reigns for a thousand years on the earth before the end of the world. In my view this is a mistaken interpretation and comes from a failure to see that chapter 20 begins a new section. Pre-millennialists see that Christ returns at the end of chapter 19—it is hard to miss—and then assume that chapter 20 follows on chronologically. So they teach that it is as clear as day: Christ returns before the millennium, and his return then ushers in a thousand year reign. The great CH Spurgeon was pre-millennial, as is Roger Carswell in our own day.

## Dispensationalism

This is really a subdivision of pre-millennialism, and some would say an extreme form. These good people are generally very easy to spot: whenever someone comes to the book of Revelation with charts and predictions, with dogmatism about who Gog and Magog are and where Hitler and Napoleon fit in—all that is dispensationalism. They always seem to know precisely what is going to happen! Often, too, they are the least willing of the four to recognise that there is any other possible interpretation: *they* have the timetable. Christian Brethren were (and still are) mostly dispensational; the Schofield reference Bible notes are dispensational. Well-known (and justly popular) American Bible teacher John MacArthur is a dispensationalist. Unlike other Christians, they believe that the second coming of Christ happens in two stages: the first time he comes 'for' his saints, and takes them away from an earth that carries on—somewhat puzzled—without them for a period of time (this is the 'secret rapture); after that period (seven years) he comes again 'with' his saints, to begin his thousand year reign. Dispensationalism is itself subdivided into different—and often opposing—camps with some believing that 'the secret rapture' will occur before the great tribulation, others that it will come after.

## Post-millennialism

Post-millennialism argues that the thousand years represents a golden age of the church which may or may not last for a literal thousand years. During that (literal or not) thousand years, the influence of the gospel grows because Satan has been bound, and eventually 'the whole world' is converted; not literally every single individual, but certainly a significant majority. In support of this a post-millennialist will point to some of the parables: for example, the parable of the mustard seed (Matthew 13:31–32) where this tiny seed produces a mighty bush in which the whole earth rests. Then, after the end of the thousand years is Satan's little season (20:3, AV), a last battle, and Christ's return. Iain Murray, author of many books and instigator of the Banner of Truth trust, is post-millennial. Most of the Puritans of the 17th century held post-millennial views, as would much current evangelical Presbyterianism. The pedigree of this view is impeccable!

## A-millennialism

'A,' of course, is a prefix meaning 'without'—so it is the wrong name for this view! A-millennialists do believe in a millennium. Unlike their pre- and post- brethren, however, they are sure it does not represent a literal thousand years. Instead, they believe it is a symbolic way of referring to the whole gospel age—that time from Christ's ascension into heaven to his return to earth in glory. It is a much more straightforward view to understand and to explain, which is certainly one advantage. In the opinion of many, it has another advantage too: that of being correct!

There should be no problem with seeing the thousand years as symbolic as so much of Revelation is. In fact, every other time measurement used in Revelation is symbolic, and every other use of numbers is symbolic too. There is no reason why this should be an exception. Once chapter 20 is seen as beginning a new section, amillennialists believe, the problems of interpreting the chapter are considerably reduced, or even eliminated. William Hendriksen, Martyn Lloyd-Jones and much of current British evangelicalism line up under this banner, and it is the view taken in this book, as the reader will probably have guessed by now.

Let me take a moment to defend the idea that this thousand years is symbolic rather than literal. How many Holy Spirits are there? One, of course. But Revelation 1:4 speaks of the seven spirits of God. Why? Because the numbers in Revelation are symbolic, seven speaks of perfection and therefore 'the seven spirits of God' reminds us that the one Holy Spirit is a perfect, even divine, being. The number seven is symbolic.

Were there are only seven churches in Asia (1:4)? No; we know that there were other churches in Asia, some of them very close to the seven churches that are dealt with in chapters 2 and 3. Why then are only these seven churches mentioned in the book? Because seven is symbolic and speaks of completion. The seven churches therefore represent the whole church of Jesus, and the letters to the seven churches are relevant for every local church in every age.

Are there only 144,000 in heaven, (14: 3)? By no means. It is a symbolic number. Twelve Jewish tribes multiplied by twelve Christian apostles gives 144. Then ten times ten times ten gives a thousand, representing a vast number: so the 144,000 symbolically tells us that there are a vast number of people, from both Old and New Testament ages, in heaven.

Numbers in apocalyptic literature are always symbols. So all the numbers in Revelation are symbolic numbers, and we have no grounds when we get into chapter 20 to decide that this number alone is not symbolic.

Sometimes, dispensationalists will say that they are the only ones who take chapter 20 seriously, but the truth is that even our most literal dispensationalist friends recognise that there is symbolism here. They see that the key (verse 1) is symbolic, and the abyss is symbolic and the chain is symbolic (a spiritual being like Satan cannot be bound with a literal chain). They know that the serpent is a symbol of the devil. Why then *insist* that the thousand years must be taken literally? It is another symbol.

I take it then that this thousand years represents the whole period between Christ's first and second coming. The whole period, that is, except for one very brief period that we will see referred to at the end of verse 3. It is called in the NIV a short time and it has become known as 'Satan's little season' because of the way it is referred to in the AV.

## Objection

Elsewhere in Revelation we have seen this period—the gospel period—designated as 'time, times and half a time'—three and a half years. Why should it suddenly now be represented as a thousand years? Because symbols are like that; they do not need to be consistent. Hell, for example, is symbolised in Scripture both as fire and as outer darkness. Fire and darkness are in reality mutually exclusive, but not when they are used as symbols. Why does John change the symbol here? Perhaps God through him here is warning us here that the gospel period—though from the perspective of heaven is only a short time (three and a half years)—will, from an earthly perspective be a very long time. So the figure of a thousand years is introduced to correct any mistaken optimism.

I am arguing here then that chapter 20 gives us yet one more representation of that whole period of history from Christ's coming right up to (almost) the very end. We have seen other such representations and this is one more. Then chapters 21 and 22 will introduce us to the glories of the new heavens and the new earth. So let us turn to chapter 20.

But just before we do let us remember: this part of the Bible, like the rest, is God's word. It is without error in all that it declares. The same is not true, of course, of my interpretation of it. You who read do not have a *right* to question my interpretation, you have a *duty* to do so! Pastors and preachers and writers of books are not infallible; only the Bible is. 'Test everything; hold on to the good' (1 Thessalonians 5:21) is a duty for us all. With that in mind, let us come to the passage itself. There are three main things in the passage: Satan bound, Satan released and Satan defeated.

## Satan bound

'I saw an angel coming down out of heaven, having the key to the Abyss and holding in his hand a great chain. He seized the dragon, that ancient serpent, who is the devil, or Satan, and bound him for a thousand years. He threw him into the Abyss, and locked and sealed it over him, to keep him from deceiving the nations any more until the thousand years were ended' (20:1–3). So Satan is cast into a great pit and bound in order to keep him from deceiving the nations. What does this binding of Satan mean?

A fundamental rule in interpreting the Bible is that Scripture must always interpret Scripture. There is only one other place in the Bible that uses the word 'bind' of Satan, and that is Matthew 12:28–29. Here the Lord Jesus Christ says 'But if I drive out demons by the Spirit of God, then the kingdom of God has come upon you. Or again, how can anyone enter a strong man's house and carry off his possessions unless he first ties up the strong man? Then he can rob his house.' 'Ties up' in verse 29 is the same Greek word translated as 'binds' in Revelation 20, and the coming of the kingdom of God is identified with the binding of 'a strong man.' The Lord Jesus is the one who has come to rob the strong man, Satan. Now, when did the Lord Jesus Christ win his victory over Satan? Plainly, on the cross; the cross is therefore the binding of the 'strong man armed'. Our Lord Jesus Christ 'binds' Satan in order to carry off his possessions—that is, in order to set free those who believe in Jesus. So, if we use the good rule of letting Scripture interpret Scripture, Jesus' use of the phrase 'binding the strong man armed' will be allowed to tell us what it means in Revelation 20 and we will not go far wrong.

Without using the same word, there is (as we have seen) another reference to the binding of Satan in Revelation 12. There (verse 8) we see Satan cast out of heaven. As we saw, that is not something that happened 'pre-history'; rather, it is something that happened when our Lord Jesus Christ went to the cross and defeated Satan. We saw that his power was greatly reduced as a result of the cross, and this passage speaks of the same thing: a binding of Satan—a reduction of his power—so that, in particular, he would 'deceive the nations no more.'

It is this phrase in particular that causes pre-millennial Christians (and post-millennial, too) to take exception to the interpretation I am giving. 'You have got to be joking,' they say. 'How can you look at the history of the last two thousand years and seriously suggest that Satan is bound, and that he is not deceiving the nations anymore. Look at the nations! Look at the world! Look how the kings and rulers of the world say 'We will not have this man to be king over us.' Look how they say of God and his Christ (in the words of Psalm 2) 'Let us break their chains.' Of course Satan is still deceiving the nations! How on earth can you say otherwise?'

But with respect to my friends, this displays a rather astonishing ignorance of what has happened since the death and resurrection of the Lord Jesus Christ. How different things are now than they used to be! Imagine that it is 50BC, and you have been travelling throughout the world looking for worshippers of the one true God. Where would you have found them? Would they be in Athens, the intellectual centre of the world? Or in Rome, the political centre of the world? No. You would have found them only in Israel, a very tiny and insignificant nation. (If there were any true worshippers in Athens or Rome, they would still have been Jews—exiles from Israel.) Then comes the Lord Jesus Christ into the world. He goes to the cross and dies, he rises from the dead and ascends into heaven. His last task before he returns into heaven is to commission his disciples to spread the gospel throughout the world and his first task from heaven is to give them the power to do it. So the apostles begin the work. Peter is the great apostle to the Jews, and Paul the great apostle to the Gentiles ('the nations'). Yet even before Paul begins his ministry, the gospel begins to spread to the non-Jewish world. The Ethiopian eunuch (Acts 8:26ff.) is a God-fearer; he seems to have had some knowledge of God before he meets Philip. But Philip meets him, explains about Jesus to him, and the Ethiopian believes and is baptised. He becomes a new creature in Christ, and goes off home to Ethiopia—and presumably he begins to speak about Christ there.

A little after this, in Acts 10, the Gentile Cornelius is converted through the ministry of Peter. And it is shortly after this that the newly-converted Paul begins his phenomenally effective missionary career. By the time he writes to the Romans (probably around 56AD, only twenty-five years or so after the ascension) he can talk about having 'fully proclaimed the gospel of Christ' to a vast arc of Asia and what we now call Europe as well (Romans 15:19). By the time we reach 350 AD, if we were travelling through the world looking for worshippers of the one true God, where would we find them? All over the world and in all the nations! Once, all the nations were deceived and salvation belonged only to one tiny, insignificant nation—the Jews. No-one else was saved! Everyone else was in bondage to the Evil One. But since Calvary and Pentecost, what a change there has been. Now the gospel spreads throughout the world. It even reaches that wet, cold, dreary island on the western extremity of the Roman Empire, Britain! And by the time we get into the 21st century, there are missionary organisations with stations in virtually every nation we can think of. There are no longer 'nations' to be reached, only tribes. Satan's power and influence have been greatly curtailed, and the gospel is gaining in strength as people of every tribe and nation and language confess joyfully that Jesus is Christ, and Christ is Lord! That, I submit, is evidence that Satan has been bound. Few of us are Jews by birth, and if we are not Jews, then we are only saved because Satan is bound.

One further evidence that this is what is meant will have to suffice. When Jesus said 'I saw Satan fall like lightning from heaven' (Luke 10:18), it was to those of his followers who had just returned from missionary activity. Jesus regards the spread of the gospel as the result of the binding of Satan.

That binding will come to an end for a short time, we are told at the end of verse three. Before we consider that, though, we need to notice that in the following verses, John shifts the focus again.

## A glimpse of heaven: saints reigning

John has told us what is happening on earth: Satan is bound, and the gospel is spreading. That is certainly good news, but it is also true that Christians are dying. What happens to them? John tells us that he sees thrones in heaven, and on the thrones are those who have been given authority to judge. We know that this is the saints: 'Do you not know that we will judge angels?' it says in 1 Corinthians 6:2–3. These thrones therefore represent living Christians—those who are already kings and priests to God (1:6). We will return to these in a moment.

But John also sees 'the souls of those who had been beheaded,'—that is, those who died in the service of Jesus. Notice, he sees their souls, not their bodies. The End has not come so they have not been resurrected bodily. (It is true that in the Bible sometimes 'soul' means person; for example we are told that seventy souls went down into Egypt (Genesis 46:27, AV and literally). But whenever that is the case, we can remove the word 'soul' from the sentence and put in 'person' or 'people' in its place. We cannot do that here. We cannot say 'I saw the people of those who had been beheaded because of the testimony of Jesus.' It would make no sense. Yes, sometimes, the Bible uses 'soul' to represent the whole person, but not always. We have a similar custom in English: when we speak, for example, of 'A hundred head of cattle,' we do not mean severed heads! We mean a hundred bulls and cows. But sometimes we do use 'head' in a narrower sense as distinct from the body. Here 'soul' is used in that way—the soul as distinct from the body.)

Notice how careful Scripture is to assure us of the safety of those Christian believers who have died. It is not enough for John to say that living Christian believers reign with Christ, but he assures us also that that privilege also belongs to Christian believers who have died. This is important because many of us have lost believing loved ones, and know the ache that it produces. We often ask 'Why?' But it is not just the 'why' question that concerns us. It is also 'where?' Where are they now? What are they doing? Lift your hearts, says John in effect. They are reigning on the thrones of heaven with Christ their Lord. They reign with Christ until the very end. We may wish them back, but they would not come back if they could.

But it is not just that those who have died in Christ who reign with him; we *all* reign with him! This is because we have all partaken of the first resurrection.

## The first resurrection

What then is this first resurrection, mentioned in verse 5? ('(The rest of the dead did not come to life until the thousand years were ended.) This is the first resurrection.') A proper understanding of this phrase is a key to the whole of the chapter.

Although this precise phrase is only used here, I have no doubt that it refers to conversion. More accurately, it speaks of regeneration—the giving of spiritual life to those who are dead in trespasses and sins (as non-Christians are described in Ephesians 2). Colossians also describes Christians as those who 'have been raised with Christ ...' (3:1). Once they were 'dead'; now they are alive—they have experienced 'the first resurrection.'

John 5 also speaks of conversion as a kind of resurrection. Jesus says: 'Just as the Father raises the dead and gives them life, even so the Son gives life to whom he is pleased to give it' (verse 21). Verse 24 continues 'I tell you the truth whoever hears my word and believes him who sent me has eternal life and will not be condemned; he has crossed over from death to life. I tell you the truth a time is coming *and has now come* when the dead will hear the voice of the Son of God and those who hear will live.' There, Jesus virtually defines the first resurrection. It is a time that is coming 'and has now come'; the preaching of the gospel raises the spiritually dead.

Furthermore, Jesus actually differentiates this from what we normally think of as 'the resurrection of the dead' in verse 28: 'Do not be amazed at this because a time is coming when all who are in their graves will hear his voice and come out.' In this passage then our Lord Jesus Christ speaks of two resurrections. One resurrection—the one we normally think of—is at the end of time when all who are in their graves will hear him and rise. But before that, there is another resurrection: when people hear the voice of the Son of God and some who hear that voice will live. Even during the life of our Lord, that time 'has now come': men and women hear the gospel of Jesus and they come—spiritually—to life. The first resurrection is being born again, and those who are born again live and reign with Christ.

This brings us back, as I promised, to the reign of living believers. Even while we still live, says Ephesians (2:6) we are seated in heavenly places with Christ. It is not something that will happen to me one day when I die; it is already true of me. John is making the same point here in Revelation 20. I am in the heavenlies with Christ. At this moment I live and reign with

Christ, and when I come to die, my soul will be in heaven and will continue to reign with Christ throughout the thousand years—the gospel age. (So will yours, if you are a Christian!) It is because of the first resurrection.

Those who have part in that first resurrection, says verse 6, are those over whom the second death has no power. They will be priests of God and of Christ and will reign with him for a thousand years. The second death is the death of eternal condemnation, and those who have been born again are those whom eternal condemnation can never touch. The first death—physical death—only changes their location, not their status. The second death—eternal condemnation—does not touch them at all.

## Satan released

However, back on earth, the gospel will not know unbroken success. In fact, when the thousand years are over, Satan will be released from his prison and go out to deceive the nations again. We do not know why God will allow this release; we are not told. We know that God is always in control, even of Satan, and we know that sometimes—for good and wise purposes—God allows evil to prosper. We have seen this little period referred to already also, in different terms. Chapter 11 has told us of three and a half days at the end of the three and a half years; a time when evil will spread. So we know that before the last day there will be a period of great opposition to the gospel. It is the time of the Antichrist, the time of the man of sin.

## Antichrist?

In his letters, John tells us that the Antichrist is coming, and that many antichrists have already come (1 John 2:18). Anyone who denies that Jesus is the Christ, for example (1 John 2:22) is the antichrist. There have always been many who deny Jesus; there have always been many antichrists.

But the one John calls 'antichrist' Paul calls 'the man of sin (or 'lawlessness') in 2 Thessalonians 2:1–12, and there is one great, final Antichrist to come at the end of the age. For the moment, says Paul, something (2 Thessalonians 2:6) and someone (verse 7) is holding him back. But the day will come when that someone will be taken out of the way, and the Antichrist will be revealed. He will exalt himself against everything that is godly, setting himself up 'in God's temple' and proclaiming himself to be God (verse 4). Since it is Christian believers who in the New Testament are regarded as God's temple, this seems to point to the church itself being deceived by this false Christ. All this, it seems, will occur immediately prior to the End.

At the end of the gospel age, Satan will be given a little season, a brief release from the abyss, a time when his power increases and he is rampant. He begins to deceive the nations again: the spread of the gospel is apparently halted. Though the church cannot be destroyed, she becomes ineffective. That brief season then brings about the terrifying spectacle of a Last Battle, here represented as against Gog and Magog.

Do not be deceived by those who try to work out which nations are meant by 'the four corners of the earth.' It is a phrase which represents all the world for all the world is gathered together in opposition. Specifically, who are Gog and Magog? It is a reference to Ezekiel 38 and 39, where Ezekiel prophesies the terrible persecution that was to come under Antiochus Epiphanes, the ruler of Syria. In about 170 BC there was an astonishing onslaught against godliness in Israel and ferocious persecution broke out. It was very brief: it was only a little season. Yet while it lasted it was ferocious indeed. Gog in Ezekiel is the evil prince of Magog—or Syria—and because the persecution was both fierce and brief, the names are used here to symbolise the last great outbreak of evil. Once again, therefore, Old Testament imagery is brought into the New Testament to represent something which is still to come. It is a time when the armies of the world will gather against God. Opposition will be world-wide and things will look bleak indeed for the church of Jesus, but it is the last attack of the forces of evil against the church.

Remember we are in a symbolic book. We do not need to think of literal armies gathering by a river, ready to fight against God. This is not a literal battle that is to happen here on the earth. Rather, it speaks of a time of vast opposition to the church. Then suddenly, when it looks as if the church cannot possibly survive, it all comes to an end.

These armies of wickedness have marched across the breadth of the earth, they have surrounded the camp of God's people, the city he loves. They settle down for a siege. They are confident of victory, sure that the church will be destroyed. Even the church expects a long battle—but suddenly it is all over. Fire comes from heaven and devours them. Perhaps you can bear a very trivial illustration? There is a scene in the film 'The Raiders of the Lost Ark' where the whip-carrying Indiana Jones is confronted by a black-clad figure, the embodiment of evil. The figure is twirling his sword masterfully, and we expect Jones to go into a long battle. We have seen him fight with his whip before and we expect it to happen again. But this time there is no prolonged fight. Instead, Indiana Jones (in a scene that had audiences applauding all over the world) simply pulls out a revolver and shoots the bad guy—and the whole film moves on. It is a poor picture of what is described here. The forces of evil have gathered and it looks as if there will be a tremendous battle. We expect that the battle will ebb and flow, first one way and then the other. But it is not what happens! The Lord of glory has had enough and fire descends from heaven and destroys his enemies with blazing fire. The same event is described in 2 Thessalonians 2:

'Concerning the coming of our Lord Jesus Christ and our being gathered to him, we ask you, brothers, not to become easily unsettled or alarmed by some prophecy, report or letter supposed to have come from us, saying that the day of the Lord has already come. Don't let anyone deceive you in any way, for that day will not come until the rebellion occurs and the man of lawlessness is revealed, the man doomed to destruction. He will oppose and will exalt himself over everything that is called God or is worshipped, so that he sets himself up in God's temple, proclaiming himself to be God. Don't you remember that when I was with you I used to tell you these things? And now you know what is holding him back, so that he may be revealed at the proper time. For the secret power of lawlessness is already at work; but the one who now holds it back will continue to do so till he is taken out of the way. And then the lawless one will be revealed, whom the Lord Jesus will overthrow with the breath of his mouth and destroy by the splendour of his coming.'

Comparing this passage carefully with what is said here in Revelation 20 helps, I believe, underline the correctness of this interpretation.. There is a period of restrained opposition—'the secret power of lawlessness is already at work' but is being held back. That restraint will be removed

(Satan's little season begins) and there will be a final revolt, with the man of lawlessness setting himself up against God and godliness. But it will not last: the Lord Jesus will overthrow him suddenly, with the breath of his mouth and the splendour of his coming. What Paul describes factually, John describes in pictures and symbols.

## Satan defeated

The overthrow of Satan and his cohorts is followed by eternal torment. Verses 10–15 describe the final end of Satan. 'The devil, who deceived them, was thrown into the lake of burning sulphur, where the beast and the false prophet had been thrown. They will be tormented day and night for ever and ever' (verse 10). In one sense the whole book of Revelation has been about this; in fact the whole Bible is about this! It is the time that the demons spoke of to our Lord Jesus: 'Have you come here to torture us before *the appointed time* …?' (Matthew 8:29). Revelation is now describing for us what those demons called 'the appointed time', but even during the ministry of Jesus the demons already knew that their doom was certain.

Now comes the judgement as a great white throne appears. The appearance is so awesome that all of heaven and earth flee before him who sits on the throne. But though the universe recoils at his splendour, all the dead are gathered before him. There are no exceptions. The sea gives up its dead, death and Hades give up their dead. Every person stands before God in judgement. To be a little more precise, it is God the Son seated on the throne for the Father has entrusted all judgement to him (see John 5:22 and Matthew 25:31–32). Everyone stands before him, and the books are opened (verse 12). Very importantly, after 'books' are opened, *another* book is opened, the Book of Life. The dead are judged according to what they have done that is recorded in the books, and John is telling us that as judgement begins, everyone's name is checked to see if it is in the Book of Life. If they are, it is all that needs to be said about them: redeemed, justified, forgiven. For those who are not there, it is the record of the other books that is checked. These people are judged according to how they have lived, what they have done. Then each of them is judged—and punished—according to their deeds. Those whose names are not in the Book of Life (verse 15) are thrown into the lake of fire. Once more we are back to the awesome judgement that we have seen so many times. We are reminded that the world's view of every man being judged in the balances—good deeds and bad weighed in opposing balances—is in one sense a perfectly Biblical view. The trouble is, no sinner has any good deeds: the very best deed is polluted by sin. All those whose names are not written in the Lamb's Book of Life always have enough written about them in 'the books' for them to be damned, to be thrown into the lake of fire. That of course is why God gave his Son to be the Saviour. If there had been people 'good enough' to earn their way into heaven, Jesus need never have died. If ever we think there are those who are good enough for heaven by their own deeds, we insult the wisdom and the grace of God as well as the cross-work of our Lord Jesus Christ who came to die and save those who could not be saved in any other way.

Then, finally, 'Death and Hades were thrown into the lake of fire.' Death itself is destroyed! What is death? It is the eternal separation of body and soul. But now all the dead have been raised, and souls and bodies are together again for all eternity.

Reunited spirits and bodies are cast into the lake of fire and death itself is destroyed. There is no escape. It is not death we should fear, but the second death. The lake of fire is the second death, and anyone whose name is not found written in the Book of Life is thrown into that lake.

But let us end the chapter with good news. The lake of fire is the second death, but for those who have part in the first resurrection, the second death has no power. If you have been raised with Christ—that is, born again by the Spirit of God—the lake of fire has no power over you. It has no place for you. Your name is in the Lamb's Book of Life, and you are pardoned. You are redeemed, and even now seated in the heavens. Your soul will be in the heavenlies when your body dies. When the end of the age comes, and all who are in their graves hear the voice of the Lord Jesus, and come out to live again, then your soul and body will be reunited and you will be in heaven, in the heaven of heavens, the paradise of God, the new city, the new Jerusalem. You will be the bride of Christ, and there will be no more crying or tears or sorrow. More of that in our final chapter!

# The city and the bride

Please read Revelation 21 and 22

In our previous chapter, we came at last to the great Day of Judgement itself and saw the judgement of God unfold. Now we come to chapters 21 and 22, where we are taken beyond the judgement. The Day of the Lord is the Last Day—but it is not the last thing that ever happens. There is a time beyond the Day of Judgement; there is a heaven beyond it. So, in these two final chapters of Revelation, we are taken beyond judgement to see heaven itself, the eternal dwelling place of the righteous. We are shown—still in symbols—what the eternal state is like.

What do I mean by 'the eternal state'? When a believer dies, his soul goes straightaway to be with the Lord (2 Corinthians 5:8, for example). We saw in Revelation 20 that they are represented as reigning with Christ throughout the whole gospel age. When an unbeliever dies, however, his soul goes straight to hell (Luke 16:23 for example). The believer is in heaven, the unbeliever in hell. In each case it is only their souls, not their bodies and this is called the intermediate state.

But when the Lord Jesus returns, there is a resurrection of the bodies of both unbeliever and believer. In each case, their souls and bodies are reunited for ever. But neither of them changes their dwelling: the believer is still in heaven (or, at any rate, the new heavens and new earth) and the unbeliever still in hell. This is what I mean by 'the eternal state' which is represented for us—in symbols—in these chapters.

Why in symbols? Without symbols I doubt very much whether we could understand. How could creatures of flesh and blood understand the eternal realities of what is to come? So we are given the information we need in symbols that speak to our hearts and enable us to grasp more of the reality than mere statements would. In that way, these symbols are not like the parables of Jesus. Do you remember being told—at school, perhaps—that Jesus spoke in parables so that everyone could understand him? Actually, that is not the case. Jesus says quite clearly in Matthew 13:10–11 that he taught in parables so that people would *not* understand him. The parables of Jesus are ways of hiding the truth, and unfolding it only to those that God has chosen. 'To you it is given to understand,' says the Lord Jesus Christ, 'But to those outside I speak only in parables so that they might be ever hearing but never understanding, ever looking but never seeing.'

But these symbols are not like that. These symbols are made to help us understand as much as we, in our earthly, unglorified state, could ever understand about the glory of heaven. So we are shown heaven as a city with a river in it and we can understand that. Again, we are shown God's people in heaven as a bride, resplendent on her wedding day. We can understand that, too. Then, as we move into chapter 21 we see the new heaven and the new earth. The first heaven and earth—the first creation— has gone away. It is passed. Peter tells us (2 Peter 3) how it will end: the universe will be wrapped up just as a tent is wrapped up and packed away. The heavens themselves will melt in fervent heat. Elsewhere (1 Thessalonians 4:16) we are told our Lord Jesus Christ will descend from heaven with a loud command to usher in the judgement for he is the one who will close the evil age in which we live.

Then there will be a new universe, a new creation—and the characteristic thing about that new creation is that sin has gone. There is no more sin at all. This is spelled out for us later, but we are given a hint of that at the end of verse 1. 'There was no longer any sea.' What—you may ask— has the sea got to do with sin? Just this: the Jewish people characteristically did not like the sea. In the book of Psalms, for example, the sea is generally portrayed in stormy conditions—in chaos with high winds and waves. For the Jews, the sea was a place that enemies came from; here in Revelation, it is the place the beast comes out of. The sea therefore symbolises trouble, chaos and—therefore—sin itself. But all of that belongs to the old order, and it has all gone away. There is to be no more sin. Instead, the holy city, the new Jerusalem, comes down out of heaven. The city of Babylon symbolised the world in its rebellion against God, but Jerusalem always symbolises the presence of God. Here it is, then; the new Jerusalem coming down from heaven, from God.

But it is a strange city, because it is also a bride, a bride beautifully dressed and fully prepared for the bridegroom, the Lord Jesus. This city is not a place where the people of God live. This city *is* the people of God. Babylon was a harlot—do you remember that we saw that when looking at chapter 17?—signifying the filth of life lived without God. The new Jerusalem though is the bride of Christ. Who are the bride of Christ? Those who by faith are forgiven their sins and taken into heaven. The city is the bride and the bride is a people. The people do not live in the New Jerusalem, they *are* the New Jerusalem!

In this city there will be no sorrow. 'The dwelling of God is now with men,' a loud voice from heaven proclaims. That most intimate of relationships, between the Son and the Bride, begins.

It is just here that we begin to come close—as close anyway as the Bible will let us—to answering one of the most frequently asked questions, the question 'why?' Why did God create the universe? Why did God create the earth? Why did he allow sin to begin, and why does he allow it to continue? Why is he working through his purposes so slowly? The nearest the Bible gives us to an answer to that kind of question is that God had it in mind to create the universe for his Son, and in that universe to prepare a Bride for his Son. For God's great purpose to be fulfilled, the glory of Jesus as Redeemer had to be shown, and so sin, the Fall and redemption all had to happen. That is as near as we can get to an answer. Now, at last, that purpose is complete and the whole universe is able to sing 'Here comes the Bride.'

Because it is a bride and a wedding, it is a time of joy. In one very important way, though, this is different from all other weddings. They have only ever been shadows, but this is the reality. This time of joy will go on for ever and ever. 'He will wipe away every tear from their eyes. There will be no more death or mourning or crying or pain ...' (verse 4) because all of those things belonged to the old order, and 'the old order of things has passed away.'

Even more, the One on the throne says 'I am making everything new' (verse 5). When we see the size of the city in verse 16, it is 12,000 stadia long—that is, about 1400 miles. It is a little further than from London to Athens; it is a big city. But the significance is not the size, but the shape. It is laid out like a square, we are told—it is as long as it is wide. But it is also as high as it is long, so it is a perfect cube. Why is this significant? Because there is only one other perfect cube described in the Bible, and that is the Most Holy Place, the Holy of Holies.

The Holy of Holies was the innermost room of first the tabernacle and then the temple. Both the tabernacle and the temple had various courts, with different people 'filtered out' at each stage, and fewer and fewer people being allowed inside. But no-one at all was allowed into the innermost room where the ark of the covenant was, where the shekinah-glory of God revealed his presence. No-one, that is, except the High Priest, and even he was allowed inside only once a year on the great Day of Atonement. Sin had separated mankind from God, and so a great heavy veil covered the Holy Place to represent that separation. Once only each year, the High Priest alone was allowed beyond that veil, and he had to take blood in with him as a proof that atonement had been made. Without that blood, even the High Priest would die. That Holy Place was a perfect cube; and the City that descends from heaven is perfect fulfilment of the Holy Place, so it too is a perfect cube. One of the most amazing things about the book of Revelation is the number of times it refers back to the Old Testament without even stopping to draw the reader's attention to it; God simply allows us to make these connections ourselves as we grow in knowledge.

So, what does this mean? It means what it says in verse 3: 'the dwelling of God is with men, and he will live with them. They will be his people, and God himself will be with them and be their God.' God will then dwell amongst his people.

When we see the gates of the city, they have the names of the twelve tribes of Israel written on them (verse 12). When we see its foundations, they contain the names of the twelve apostles (verse 14). Twelve tribes, twelve apostles. There are not two cities, two ways of salvation or two destinies for the saved. There is and always has been only one way of salvation, faith in the Lord Jesus Christ. Old Testament saints looked forward to him, and we look backward to him—but we all look to him. The Old Testament church and the New Testament church are in heaven together and they constitute one city.

It is an indescribably glorious city. It is made of and inlaid with jasper and sapphire and countless precious stones (verses 18–20). We do not have to know the details of these gems—only to understand that the most precious things imaginable make up the city itself.

But the glory of the city does not lie in its foundations. Its gates are pearls and a complete pearl makes each gate (21). What pearls they must be! But the glory of the city is not even in its gates.

No, the glory of the city is that the Lamb of God is in it (22). 'I did not see a temple in the city,'—obviously not, because the city itself is the innermost part of the temple. The temple always represented the presence of God with his people, but what has hitherto only been symbolised is now ultimate reality: 'the Lord God Almighty and the Lamb are its temple.' John is struggling to tell us its glory; this city does not need the sun or the moon to shine, for the glory of God gives it light, and the Lamb is its lamp.

Perhaps, though, even as we are surprised by its glories we may find ourselves wondering if it will last. We have known beautiful things before, and even tasted something of the presence of God with us. But beauty fades and passes, and even our sense of God's presence does not remain constant. Will this be any different, we may ask ourselves? True, it is very glorious. 'What a city,' we cry. 'What walls, what foundations, what gates! But how can we be sure that it will not all go horribly wrong? When God created the garden of Eden, did he not create it perfect? When he put Adam and Eve in that garden, were they not perfect? Yet they chose willingly to sin against God and bring corruption into the whole universe! Then how can we be sure it will not all happen again in this new heaven and earth?'

'Do not worry about that,' says John in effect (verse 27). 'Nothing impure will ever enter it and there is no possibility of this new creation being spoiled.' No-one who does what is shameful or deceitful will be allowed to enter, either. How was God's garden spoiled? When the Serpent (Satan) came in. He was already shameful and deceitful, a liar and the Father of lies, (John 8:44). But now he has been cast into the lake of fire, and even if another one like him could be found, there would be no entry into this city for him.

Now let us proceed into chapter 22. In the city is a river, and the river is the water of life, as clear as crystal and flowing from the throne of God and of the Lamb. It flows down the middle of the great street. It is a life-giving river, with a tree (verse 2)—the tree of life. That tree is now open to all, and not barred.

Again, this imagery refers back to the Old Testament. In Genesis

3:22–24, mankind is turned out of the garden so that they do not eat of the fruit of the tree of life and so live for ever—live for ever with sin upon them. An angelic guard is put on the garden itself, barring the way. But now the cross of Christ and the victory of God have changed all that and the tree is freely available. It is a rich tree, bearing fruit every month. It is a powerful tree—even its leaves heal the nations. Just as the tree of the knowledge of good and evil (Genesis 2:9) brought a curse to all the nations, now that curse is undone. Eve took fruit from that tree, and Adam tragically followed her lead. Ruin came on us all as a result, but now that ruin is undone.

In one sense, the Bible is a story of three trees: the tree of the knowledge of good and evil, the tree of Calvary, and the tree of life. By hanging on Calvary's tree, our Lord Jesus Christ took the curse that belonged to our race for eating from the first tree and gave us access at last to the third. The curse is reversed and the nations are no longer spoiled, but healed. No curse remains.

## Parallels

Many commentators have stressed the parallels between the opening chapter of Genesis and the book of Revelation.

Genesis tells us that God created heaven and earth. Revelation describes the *new* heaven and earth (21:1). In Genesis the luminaries are called into being: sun, moon and stars. In Revelation we read: 'And the city has not need of the sun, nor of the moon, to shine in it; for the glory of God lightened it, and its lamp is the Lamb' (21:23). Genesis describes a paradise which was lost. Revelation pictures a paradise restored (Rev.2:7; 22:2). Genesis describes the cunning and power of the devil. The Apocalypse tells us that the devil was bound and hurled into the lake of fire and brimstone. Genesis pictures that awful scene of man fleeing away from God and hiding himself from the presence of the Almighty. Revelation shows us the most wonderful and intimate communion between God and redeemed man… Finally, whereas Genesis shows us the tree of life, with an angel to keep the way to the tree of life, 'lest man put forth his hand and take of its fruit', the Apocalypse restores to man his right to have access to it: 'that they may have the right to come to the tree of life' (22:14).[1]

So it is that God the master author wraps up every loose end in the plot.

Nothing is left dangling and no thread is there for us to pull at and say 'That doesn't quite fit.' It is all a master plot, a masterpiece indeed. The point of it is: at last the dwelling of God is with his people, and they see his face, and there is no night. These words, says the angel, are faithful, trustworthy and true (verse 6).

## Closing exhortations

All that remains now is for us to glance at some closing exhortations. There are three we must notice.

The *first* is a very specific exhortation to John, to worship God and him alone, (22:9). In verse 8 we are told that he fell down to worship at the feet of the angel that had been showing him these things, but the angel rebuked him: 'Do not do it! I am a fellow servant with you and with your brothers the prophets and of all who keep the words of this book.' John has misunderstood what he has just heard. Hearing the voice in verse 7, which is certainly the Lord Jesus Christ, he assumes that the angel who has been showing him the visions is the Lord, too. But he is wrong. This angel, great though he is, is only a servant. This is important because heretical groups love to point to verse 9 and argue 'The one speaking in verse 9 is the same one as the one speaking in verse 7. It is Jesus in verse 7, and in verse 9 he says 'Do not worship me …!' But look again and you will see it is not so. The voice of verse 9 and the voice of verse 7 are not from the same person. We know that because the truth is made clearer in verse 16: 'I, Jesus, *have sent my angel* to give you this testimony for the churches.' So although the voice in verse 7 comes from the surroundings, it is not the voice of the angel. It is a different voice. We have already seen something similar in chapter 1: God speaks to the Son, the Son speaks to the angel and the angel speaks to John. That is exactly what we are told again here. It is not the Lord Jesus who refuses worship—and why should he? Has not the book of Revelation told us that the throne of God is the throne of the Lamb? Has not even this chapter (verse 1) told us that? There is one throne in heaven, and the Lamb sits upon it. Even on earth, when Jesus was worshipped he accepted it (e.g. John 20:28); he knows it is his due.

The *second* exhortation is a strange one: 'Let him who does wrong continue to do wrong; let him who is vile continue to be vile; let him who does right continue to do right; and let him who is holy continue to be holy' (verse 11). What does that mean? The great nineteenth-century evangelist D.L. Moody thought he knew. When someone asked him what the Bible had to say about smoking, Moody advised him to continue, on the basis of this verse, which in the Authorised Version reads 'He which is filthy, let him be filthy still.' I think we can reject that interpretation! (And I think we can be sure even Moody was jesting!)

The clue to understanding the meaning of this strange verse is to take it with verse 10. God is telling us that he is drawing a line under human history; it is coming to an end. Even as the end of history arrives, there are some who do wrong, in spite of all that is written even in the book of Revelation. Well, now it is time to let them continue. If they will not hear the words of this prophecy, leave them alone. There is nothing more to say. If they are determined to perish, then perish they will, and perish they must. But those who seek righteousness and holiness—let them alone too, for they will live. 'Behold, I am coming soon, and my reward is with me.' How foolish for any of us not to live in the light of this! How easily people make their excuses. 'Oh, life is so busy. There is so much to do, and I have so little time. I cannot fit God in, even if I would like to.' Sin can certainly be pleasurable and the Bible admits as much (see Hebrews 11:25). But its pleasures are only ever for a short time, and those who will not surrender the pleasures are fools indeed. There is a heavenly city, and all who do wrong are outside of it. 'Well,' says another, 'the standards of God are so high that all I can do is hope for mercy. I really could not live like that. I'm not sure I would want to—but even if I did want to, I could never keep it up. I can only hope that God is not as severe as you say he is.' Be assured; there is no mercy for those who will not leave their sin. That is what the angel is saying. He tells us (verse 15) that those who do wrong will be kept outside the city. 'Well,' says a third, 'I have got my faith in Christ. I believe all that you believe. I just cannot see the point of all this devotion, and all this struggling to be righteous. Why can we not just bend a little? Do we really have to be so straight? Can we not afford to be a little fuzzy around the edges?' But no, says this chapter. 'I will give to everyone according to what he has done,' says Jesus (12). It is certainly not enough to be 'righteous,' to be moral and yet not to have faith. We cannot save ourselves. But on the other hand the Bible makes it clear that it is certainly not enough either 'just' to believe, and not to be righteous.

Let no-one think that by saying this I am denying the Bible truth of justification by faith alone. Let me make this as clear as I can: the only way we can be saved is by faith alone in the Lord Jesus Christ alone. Faith is the channel by which blessing comes to us and the death of Jesus and his righteousness are the grounds on which God acquits us. It is only faith that can act as the channel, bringing God's blessing to us. We are saved, justified, by faith alone without the works of the law (see Romans 3:28). Righteousness and morality have nothing to do with our acceptance with God at all. That is good, because our righteousness has no solid ground on which we could build a ladder to heaven. There is not even a tiny piece of ground—as if we could place our ladder with one leg on faith and one on righteousness. Not at all!

But—and it is a 'but' present in the teaching of Paul, and of James, and here in Revelation too—the faith which saves, transforms. Those who are not radically transformed do not have saving faith. They may believe, but it is the wrong kind of belief. In their sense, the devil also believes—and shudders (James 2:19).

After more than twenty years' pastoral experience, I know that this truth worries many of the most godly. It is not that they do not believe it; they do. It is just that they see so little change in their lives—or rather, they see so much remaining sin. How can they be saved? No true preacher wants to disturb the godly unnecessarily! Nonetheless, this truth is too important to soft-pedal. In all those who trust Christ there is the beginning of a new life within them that wars against sin. They fight sin and do not give up on the battle. Though they slip and fall and cause themselves, God and others much pain, they do not end by walking away into ungodliness and justifying it to anyone who will listen. They cannot do that. 'I will give to everyone according to what he has done,' says the Lord Jesus Christ. That is because he can see those who have faith by the way they live. That is what he is saying here. God will not give you according to what you say, but according to what you do. You have confessed Christ and that is a good thing. Do you live Christ? For if you do not, your confession is empty. If you practise magic arts or are immoral or a murderer or an idolater or a liar you will be outside the city, says verse 15. You will be in the lake of fire (21:8). Nor should we think we will escape because 'our' sin is not there—if, for example, you were a thief but not a liar. That is not the point. Those who do not do righteousness cannot inherit the kingdom of God. We cannot fool God, and what we sow we will reap.

The *third* and final exhortation follows. How do we react to this message of Revelation? Certainly we must say with verse 20, 'Amen! Come Lord Jesus.' And he is coming soon; the Spirit yearns for that and the Bride yearns for that. But before we say 'Yes, come Lord Jesus,' there is another invitation we must give. 'The Spirit and the bride say, "Come!" And let him who hears say, "Come!" Whoever is thirsty, let him come; and whoever wishes, let him take the free gift of the water of life' (verse 17). The Bride—that is, the church—empowered by the Spirit takes the gospel command, the gospel invitation, into all the world. That is what we are for.

So we say to the world, 'Whoever is thirsty, let him come. And whoever wishes, let him take the free gift of the water of life.' It is a free gift. We offer that gift to those who want it—anyone! In his closing moments on earth (Matthew 28:19–20) Jesus commanded his disciples to take the gospel into the world. Now, right on the closing page of the Bible the gospel invitation goes out again.

For it is amazing grace, but God's last word to the world is not verse 11—let him who does wrong continue to do wrong. His last word is 'O! Give up your sin! O come, take the free gift of the water of life.' Is not this truly amazing? The very first thing God did when Adam and Eve fell into sin was to slaughter an animal (Genesis 3:21) and give them skin to cover their nakedness. This was not merely clothing for a harsh climate, it was symbolic of their sin being covered. Then, almost without a pause, in Genesis 3:15 God promises a coming Saviour. Sin has only just entered the world, and already grace is showing. All the way through the Old Testament that promise is repeated as the law and the prophets and the history and the wisdom literature all point forward to Jesus. Then in the New Testament the single theme is Jesus, and every book points to him as the fulfilment of God's great promise. Now here we are at the very end of the Bible and God says 'I will just say it one more time: come.' So let me say it a third time: truly God's grace *is* amazing. He does not want us to miss what he is saying.

The flip side of this of course is that if we have to stand before the wrath of his judgement, we will never be able to say, 'But you never gave me a chance, Lord!' Every mouth is silenced at judgement (Romans 3:19); but if we *were* foolish enough to try to argue, God would point us again to this book. He would remind us that all down the ages the gospel drum has throbbed with insistent beat: Come, come, come.

A final warning follows about the danger of misusing Scripture, and the book of Revelation in particular. It is a fearful thing to misuse God's word and there are dreadful plagues written in this book and they all belong—all of them—to those who deny God's word. But let me end this book with that throbbing gospel drum: come, come, come. If you have never been converted, who is that calls you to come? It is the church, the Bride of Christ. And every time the church gives out that invitation, the Spirit is there, calling 'Come, come, come.' The kingdom of this world has become the kingdom of our God and of his Christ, and he shall reign for ever and ever. Hallelujah, for the Lord God omnipotent reigns. Come to him, and find rest for your soul.

Hear the church triumphant singing,
Worthy the Lamb.
Highest heaven with praises ringing,
Worthy the Lamb.
Thrones and power before him bending,
Odours sweet with voice ascending
Swell the chorus never ending,
Worthy the Lamb!

John Kent, 1766–1843